ABOUT ISLAND PRESS

Island Press is the only nonprofit organization in the United States whose principal purpose is the publication of books on environmental issues and natural resource management. We provide solutions-oriented information to professionals, public officials, business and community leaders, and concerned citizens who are shaping responses to environmental problems.

In 1994, Island Press celebrated its tenth anniversary as the leading provider of timely and practical books that take a multidisciplinary approach to critical environmental concerns. Our growing list of titles reflects our commitment to bringing the best of an expanding body of literature to the environmental community throughout North America and the world.

Support for Island Press is provided by The Geraldine R. Dodge Foundation, The Energy Foundation, The Ford Foundation, The George Gund Foundation, William and Flora Hewlett Foundation, The John D. and Catherine T. MacArthur Foundation, The Andrew W. Mellon Foundation, The Joyce Mertz-Gilmore Foundation, The New-Land Foundation, The Pew Charitable Trusts, The Rockefeller Brothers Fund, The Tides Foundation, Turner Foundation, Inc., The Rockefeller Philanthropic Collaborative, Inc., and individual donors.

DESIGNING THE CITY

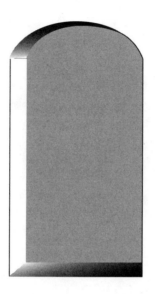

DESIGNING THE CITY

A Guide for Advocates and Public Officials

Adele Fleet Bacow

ISLAND PRESS

WASHINGTON, D.C. • COVELO, CALIFORNIA

Illustrations on pages xiii, 18, 28, 80, 84, 96, 98, 138, 141, 144, and 155 are by Lawrence E. Green and were reproduced from *Building for the Arts,* by Catherine R. Brown, William Fleissig, and William Morrish, published in 1984 (and revised and republished in 1989) by the Western States Arts Federation, Santa Fe, New Mexico; copyright © 1984, 1989 by the Western States Arts Federation. These illustrations were reprinted with permission from the artist and the publisher.

Illustrations on pages 12 through 16 are by Lawrence E. Green and were created for use in this publication.

ISLAND PRESS is a trademark of The Center for Resource Eco-nomics.

Library of Congress Cataloging-in-Publication Data

Bacow, Adele Fleet.
    Designing the city: a guide for advocates and public officials/ by Adele Fleet Bacow.
        p. cm.
    Includes bibliographical references and index.
    ISBN 1-55963-290-9 (cloth). — ISBN 1-55963-291-7 (paper)
    1. City planning—United States.   2. Community development, Urban—United States.   I. Title.
    HT167.B33   1995
    307.1'216'0973—dc20   94-30144
                                                                            CIP

Printed on recycled, acid-free paper ∞ ✿

Manufactured in the United States of America

10 9 8 7 6 5 4 3 2 1

For Larry, with infinite love

And to our best collaborative design—

Jay and Kenny.

Contents

Chapter 1

Getting Better Design in Your Community

Chapter 2

Convincing Arguments for Design

Chapter 6

INTEGRATING DESIGN INTO
FINANCE AND DEVELOPMENT

Chapter 7

REWARDING QUALITY DESIGN:
THE GOVERNOR'S DESIGN AWARDS PROGRAM

Chapter 8

EDUCATION AS ADVOCACY:
FROM PUBLIC OFFICIALS TO CHILDREN

PREFACE

Designing the City: A Guide for Advocates and Public Officials is a practical manual for citizens, policymakers, and activists who want to improve the way their communities are planned, designed, and built. I wrote this book as a response to requests from many people seeking advice on ways to improve their public environment. It is based in large part on my experience as a city planner and design advocate working with numerous state agencies, cities, and towns. Little information exists on how to work toward quality design. Many books are available on issues such as the process of design, what makes design "good" or "bad," and organizing for political change. A serious gap occurs, however, in documenting successful strategies and approaches to working with key players in the design and development process. This book helps fill that gap.

This book is not intended as an architectural treatise on design principles; numerous examples abound. Nor is it possible within the scope of this book to adequately define "good" or "bad" design. Instead, this book provides an approach to design decision making and ways to influence those decisions. In it you will find ways to make your voice heard and examples of successful strategies for working with designers, developers, and people in the public and private sectors to improve your neighborhood or community.

The goal of this book is to provide tangible and proven models and strategies to help you to:

• Establish unique and productive partnerships
• Develop resources to get your project accomplished
• Broaden your expertise, perspective, and constituency
• Increase the legitimacy of your program
• Create new and enduring models for effective action
• Educate participants and consumers of the design and development process

Here is how you might use this book: Chapter 1, "Getting Better Design in Your Community," provides an overview to design advocacy, describes various participants in the design process, and outlines effective roles for action to obtain better design. The second chapter, "Convincing Arguments for Design," offers responses to those hard questions you are asked constantly (or perhaps you are the one posing these difficult queries). The most typical perceptions and excuses offered by others as to why "it can't be done" will be raised, along with convincing answers. Chapters 3 through 8 present specific strategies and successful programs created especially for use in working with municipal and state government on tangible community design projects and educating citizens and decision makers in the process.

These approaches are extremely diverse; they include bridge and highway design, grant programs, artists' housing and cultural facility development, state finance and development agency policies on design, awards programs, and education of both public officials and children about design. All of these strategies can be adapted for your benefit on a local or state level. The final chapter, "Practical Tips for Action," will help you assess opportunities and problems, determine a plan of action, build a constituency, find the resources, anticipate the problems, and turn a good idea into action. The appendixes and bibliography provide additional information to aid in implementing many of the programs and strategies described in the text of the book.

If you opened this book, you most likely have a role in the design process or you are concerned about the future of your town. The intended audience of this book includes people with very different yet significant roles in influencing the design and development of our communities. This book is for you if you are affected by state and local government, including mayors, planning and zoning boards, legislators, public finance agencies, redevelopment authorities, environmental agencies, and public works departments who build, finance, or oversee development projects. In both the public and the private sectors, developers, financial institutions, architects, planners, engineers, and landscape designers continually work to influence the shape of our cities and towns. Other important groups who would benefit from the lessons presented in this book include community development corporations, neighborhood associations, state and local arts organizations, Chambers of Commerce and downtown improvement associations, environmental organizations, citizen advocacy groups, and concerned residents.

Many of the ideas shared in this book stem from my work as the creator and director of the Design and Development Program of the Massachusetts Council on the Arts and Humanities (now known as the Massachusetts Cultural Council). The Design and Development Program established partnerships with other state agencies involved in the development process, with cities and towns, and with citizens across the state to help improve the quality of design of the public environment. In 1988 the Design and Development Program received a Presidential Design Achievement Award as a model of design excellence. Strategies I developed at the Council (and with other state arts councils, such as Oklahoma) and the lessons learned are incorporated throughout this book. More recently I coordinated the Mayors Institute on City Design/Northeast and a new initiative integrating arts and community development for the New England Foundation for the Arts. These programs provided valuable insights which I share here. I hope that within these pages you will find ideas for action, practical tips to keep you going, and moral support for your own efforts.

Acknowledgments

The research for this book was supported by grants to the author from the Design Arts Program of the National Endowment for the Arts, a federal agency, and the New England Foundation for the Arts.

Without the challenge of creating a new program in design for the Massachusetts Council on the Arts and Humanities, I never would have had the opportunity to learn the lessons explored in this book. I am deeply grateful to the leadership of the Council for giving me this quest, particularly Anne Hawley and Holly Sidford who conceptualized the design program in the beginning and always inspired me to do more. Special recognition should be given to my colleagues in the Design and Development Department, Anne Nissen and Anne McKnight, who contributed tremendously to the early research and development of this book, as well as to the design programs described herein. My earliest collaborators, David Murray and Karen Rosenzweig Levine, were essential in the creation and implementation of the Council's Design and Development Program.

This book could not have been written without the support and encouragement from the Design Arts Program of the National Endowment for the Arts. The NEA not only provided the Design Arts Fellowship that enabled me to write this book, but its Design Arts Program supported many of the individual projects described in Chapters 3 through 8. Special thanks and appreciation are offered to Adele Chatfield-Taylor, Charles Zucker, Randy McAusland, Alan Brangman, and Wendy Clark. I also am extremely grateful for additional grant support awarded by the New England Foundation for the Arts for completion of this book.

The earliest stage of creation is always the most difficult and the most important. Pivotal to the success of the Design and Development Program were the support and leadership of Governor Michael Dukakis and Tunney Lee, former Deputy Commissioner of the Massachusetts Division of Capital Planning and Operations and Professor of Architecture and Planning at MIT. Frank Keefe, former Secretary of the Executive Office of Administration and Finance, provided important direction to other state agencies in establishing design policies. Meg Maguire of Environmental Images and Maguire/Reeder, Ltd. gave the initial and most essential technical support to me in creation of the Design and Development Program, as she has for other state arts councils around the country.

All the programs described in this book are truly collaborative efforts. My sincere thanks and appreciation are extended to my partners and collaborators in the programs we developed together: Ken Kruckemeyer, former Associate Commissioner of the Massachusetts Department of Public Works for his work on bridge design; Randall Arendt of the Center for Rural Massachusetts and technical advisor with the Rural Design Assistance Program; Lisa Safier, Coordinator of the Space Program at the Council; Kim Comart, Council legal counsel; development consultants Catherine Donaher, Rebecca Lee, Barbara Kaplan, and Jero Nesson; Mary Jane Daly, Project Director for the Governor's Design Awards Program; and Anne Mackin and Alex Krieger, authors of *A Design Primer for Cities and Towns*. Professor Mark Schuster of MIT supervised early graduate student research on public incentives for better design, and we later worked together at MIT coordinating the Mayors Institute on City Design. The Boston Society of Architects and its Executive Director Richard Fitzgerald were constant supporters of the programs mentioned in this book. In addition, each of the programs described in Chapters 3 through 8 benefited from advisory boards, panels, and experts who volunteered their time and experience to make them a success.

I also am particularly grateful to Rick Schwartz, former Director of Public Information at the Council, who was brave enough to review the earliest draft of this manuscript, and to Jonathan Barnett who gave me essential advice and encouragement on this book when I needed it the most. My good friends Doris Goldstein and Anne Mackin offered excellent editorial improvements, while Marsha Firestone and Anne McDermott provided careful proofreading. My sincere thanks extend to Beata Boodell Corcoran and Christine Saum of the Mayors Institute on City Design, who assisted me with my survey of mayors around the country and subsequent research requests, as well as to Harvard University's Loeb Fellowship in Advanced Environmental Studies, which gave me access to graduates of their program in order to tap their expertise. The National Trust for Historic Preservation and the Mayors Institute on City Design kindly approved use of the "Urban Design Glossary" included as Appendix B of this book. Susan Hyatt of Design Access provided essential research assistance in identifying NEA-funded projects around the country. I am especially appreciative of Lawrence E. Green's illustrations, which enliven the text of this book. Several of his drawings first appeared in the excellent resource *Building for the Arts,* published by the Western States Arts Federation, and others were created specifically for this book.

The manuscript was completed in Amsterdam, and I thank the Timburgen Institute for offering an inspiring locale for the difficult stage of final editing. Finally, and most importantly, I offer my thanks and love to my husband, Larry, and sons Jay and Kenny, to whom I dedicate this book.

Chapter 1

GETTING BETTER DESIGN IN YOUR COMMUNITY

Design and Development: A Dynamic Tension

Designers constantly strive for quality design. Developers look for a quality product that results in an economic return. Planners and public officials ideally seek the best for their community. No one actively seeks an ugly building or public space, so how does it happen? Cost is not always the issue but frequently receives the blame. "Expensive" does not have to be the adjective before "quality design."

The process of design and development is a dynamic tension in which numerous parties, often with different goals, priorities, budgets, and time lines, must come together. Contrary to popular opinion, the creation of our buildings, highways, parks, and public spaces occurs in much larger arenas than the drafting tables of architects and engineers. This collaborative and often conflicting process is based on the needs and desires of the client, the design team, the developer, the community, and the ultimate user. Important decisions are influenced by citizen groups, public officials, the financial community, and the media.

Design Advocates and Decision Makers

Successful advocates influence more than just the designers. They reach the decision makers who mandate what goes where in our public environment, the financial leaders who determine whether the project will be built, and the regulators who judge whether the proposed project meets complicated, often indecipherable codes and requirements. Who are these advocates and decision makers? Consider just a few examples:

- The mayor who decides whether the last parcel of waterfront land is to be used for a public park or a parking lot.
- The public works director who decides whether a new roadway going through downtown relates to the small scale of the community or the federal highway standards of interstate roadways.
- The city council which mandates that the renovation of city hall include provisions for quality landscaping, outdoor cultural events, and public art.
- The neighborhood organization which insists that the design of a new development fit the size and character of their community.
- The local or state arts agency that creates a model project or funding program in design.
- The state financing agency that creates guidelines to establish design quality as one of several project criteria prior to approval of public funds.

An advocate can be a citizen, mayor, public official, corporate executive, or agency staff member. An effective advocate knows how to generate ideas and enthusiasm, leverage resources, secure partners, solicit public advice and support, and carry on the momentum. This book presents ways to accomplish these goals and to establish effective partnerships and programs.

Clients and consumers of design also have a powerful influence. Do not underestimate the role of the "nondesigner" in the design and development process. An extremely talented designer can produce a disastrous building because the client was misguided, unreasonable, or uninformed. A mediocre designer can produce the best product of his or her career, in contrast, because an enlightened client set inspiring goals, provided useful guidance, and established proper parameters.

What Is Design Anyway?

You will see reference to the word *design* throughout this book. What exactly does it mean, and how does it influence communities or public spaces? Most importantly, what difference does it make in your day-to-day life? Who is responsible for designing these places or objects, and what role can you play to make the results better for your own purposes and for those around you?

DESIGN IS A PROCESS OF PROBLEM SOLVING
AND CREATING SOLUTIONS.

Design may be defined as *a process of problem solving and creating which results in a plan, product, idea, or place.* Design creates a solution to a particular objective or need. The result can be an object, a building, a place, a plan, or a process. Good design is derived from a clearly stated objective, exploration of various design alternatives, and evaluation of these alternatives to find a solution which best meets the stated objective effectively and elegantly. In the context of urban or environmental design, good design results in a building, landscape, or place which relates to the surrounding neighborhood while also adding creative enjoyment and use of space.

Designers give careful attention to issues such as the scale or size of the building or place in relationship to adjacent buildings and uses of space. Most importantly, good designers consider the scale and use of the project in relationship to the people inhabiting the space. The building blocks of design include form, color, type and texture of materials used, balance and symmetry (or asymmetry), height, scale, and density. Broader design issues must be explored thoroughly, such as the siting or location of the building or landscape in the area; environmental conditions such as wind, water, sun, and shade and their influence on the space; and transportation considerations such as public transit, pedestrian and vehicular access, and the relationships between different modes of transportation.

As you will see reiterated throughout this book, design is most definitely not an "afterthought," a "frill," "just aesthetics," or "something that happens after all the other more important factors are considered." Design decisions should not occur when all the other development factors are solved.

The word *design* is associated most typically with fields such as art, architecture, landscape architecture, graphics, and industrial design. Design applies to any creative endeavor, however, whether it is engineering, mathematics, science, or the arts. What is so intriguing about the design of public spaces is the involvement of virtually all the disciplines listed above, along with sociology, government, environmental studies, economics, and psychology.

The word *design* typically relates to the qualities of an object or building. In this book, however, "design" refers to the creation and improvement of buildings, public spaces, landscapes, transportation systems (ranging from a bus stop to a major highway interchange), and larger scale urban and rural spaces. You will notice a particular emphasis on the design of the public environment.

"Public environment" typically refers to spaces such as city halls, libraries, schools, sidewalks, and parks—all built, paid for, and maintained by government. The notion of public space should be broadened by including places built and maintained by the private sector but used by the public. Consider places such as outdoor plazas between office buildings, large parking garages or lots, billboards, facades of privately owned buildings along major roadways, or the interior of shopping malls. Private shopping malls, in particular, have replaced earlier town commons as meeting and socializing areas for many neighborhood residents.

Influencing Design

Public and private sector places are regulated by government through zoning and planning boards, environmental and historic review, and reliance on publicly supported transportation and utility systems. Governmental policies, technology, the economy, and citizens' preferences are powerful forces in shaping our public environment. The planners, architects, developers, and financial community have key roles.

The most basic design issue, the use of the space and the decision to create and build it in the first place, is often made by nondesigners. This fact effectively makes us all designers as we choose to create, build, buy, use, or change a building or an environment.

WE ALL BECOME DESIGNERS AS WE MAKE
DECISIONS ABOUT THE WAY WE USE,
ALTER, OR CONSUME SPACE.

WHO AFFECTS DESIGN?

CITIES AND TOWNS
Mayors, City Managers
City Councils, Boards of Selectmen
Planning Boards
Zoning Boards
Design Review Boards
Historic Preservation Agencies
Conservation Commissions
Library Commissions
Departments of Education
Transportation and Public Works Offices
Recreation Departments

STATE LEVEL
Governor and Legislature
State Planning Offices
Departments of Community Affairs or Development
Transportation Agencies
Public Works Departments
Environmental Affairs Departments
Industrial Finance Agencies
Public Housing Authorities
Historic Preservation Offices
State Financing Agencies
State Construction Agencies
State Arts Agencies

DESIGN AND DEVELOPMENT PRACTITIONERS
Developers
Community Development Corporations
Contractors and Construction Companies
Banks and Financial Institutions
Architects/Urban Designers
Landscape Architects
Urban Planners
Engineers
Professional Design Societies

OTHER KEY GROUPS
Advocacy Groups
Citizens Organizations
Educators
Major Businesses and Industries
Clients/Purchasers of Design Services or Products
Citizens as Taxpayers and Voters
Children

Who affects design in your community or your state? The list of influential people is much longer than you might imagine. Consider the organizations or individuals who play powerful roles in the public and private sectors, as summarized in the accompanying window.

Throughout this book you will see tangible and proven examples of effective advocacy for quality design. Many of the examples may serve as models for your own work or concerns. As you read through the examples, consider what role various people played. See which examples are most appropriate for your own circumstances. Perhaps you could convince decision makers in your community or state to adapt these ideas to meet your own needs.

What Can Design Accomplish?

Working as a problem solver, good design can accomplish many goals. Within the framework of design of the public environment, design can make:

- Cities more livable, enjoyable, and economically stable
- Communities and neighborhoods easier to navigate and identify
- Transportation more efficient
- Parks and recreational areas more pleasurable
- Workplaces and industries more productive and profitable
- Schools more conducive to learning
- Homes more affordable and accessible
- Farmlands more productive and stable
- Downtowns less threatening and more lively

Design is an ongoing process involving numerous participants. The process of design is iterative and never-ending. Buildings, neighborhoods, the environment, and cities (and certainly people) go through various life cycles where needs, circumstances, priorities, and patterns of living change. Each of these changes profoundly affects the public realm.

Changes in architectural and sociological trends dramatically alter preferences and patterns of living. Technological advances, changing public policies, citizen preferences, and family patterns influence growth, development, or even elimination of neighborhoods. New construction techniques and materials, for example, resulted in the development of high-rise apartment buildings as a solution for affordable housing in dense urban areas. In certain cities in the United States, this housing type later became a symbol of unsafe public housing with inordinate amounts of drug activity and crime.

Housing patterns and styles of living can change substantially from generation to generation. Movement from the urban to suburban neighborhoods is one obvious example. People who favor downtown living may scoff at their perception of suburban lifestyles, immortalized in Malvina Reynolds' folk song *Little Boxes,* sung by Pete Seeger, which describes "Little boxes on the hillside, Little boxes made of ticky tacky. . . . And they all look just the same."[1]

Staunch urbanists often change their tune when their growing children and desire for open space become more important. Other families, in contrast, renew their confidence in the inner city as historic revitalization and mixed-use development expand opportunities for living downtown, effectively eliminating long commutes to work while offering a diversity of lifestyles, housing, and access to cultural events.

Making Good Design

What is required for good design to occur? If you are the client or the consumer of design, how can you ensure that your needs are met? If you are the designer, how can you be sure you and your clients speak the same language? For both the designer and the client, talent, creativity, experience, and good judgment are essential factors in creating quality design. Not all clients and designers can excel in all those characteristics, but careful collaboration and communication can create a project that is outstanding and enduring.

GOOD CLIENTS MAKE GOOD DESIGN HAPPEN.

The following guidelines enable good design to take place. Many of these suggestions apply to the client and the advocate for quality design. The tips listed below will elicit the best results from your design and development team. Although these suggestions apply to the community design process, they also prove essential for other endeavors involving design as well.

- Ask the right questions
- Educate the leaders
- Create opportunities for success
- Find the best talent possible
- Be careful about changing the rules in the middle of the game
- Set a realistic budget, work plan, and timetable
- Involve people affected by your project
- Remember the ultimate user

Ask the right questions

Too often designers are asked to solve the wrong problem. Will a new parking garage improve the economic vitality of your downtown? A well-designed park or another mix of uses may be a better answer. Be sure you are clear as to your stated goals and objectives and be sure that you ask designers to solve the right problem. Consider the big picture, but don't neglect important details. Be sure to put your project in the context of the larger community.

Educate leaders about design

The most effective targets for advocacy are public leaders and decision makers. The commitment and leadership of municipal and state leaders toward quality design are critical factors for success. If you don't see evidence of this commitment in your leadership, adapt some of the strategies in this book to educate them. Look to their boards and most trusted staff members for allies as well.

Create opportunities for success

Decisions are made every day which influence your community. Consider ways to capitalize on existing activity to the benefit of your town. Perhaps a proposed bridge or highway could be designed with an overlook for a scenic area. A new library or town hall could include community meeting and performance space or landscaping coordinated with public art. School curricula could be adapted to include an understanding of design as a way of integrating social studies, art, and math.

Public financing programs could adapt their guidelines to include design quality as a criterion for funding. The key is to become involved *early* in the process to incorporate your goals before major decisions are made.

Find the best talent possible

Search hard for the best talent you can find for your project. Use a fair and open process for hiring consultants and staff. When hiring a design team, you won't necessarily want the most famous firm, the one with the flashiest proposal, or the one with the lowest bid. Some projects work best with an unusual combination of talent in the design team, such as designers, engineers, artists, and a sociologist or an environmental psychologist. Be sure the chemistry works among the project team and the client, and be clear about who exactly will be working on your project. (It won't always be the person giving the presentation.) Scrutinize references and work products carefully. Check references by calling former clients of the firm. Once you find talent, give them room to succeed. Be open to new ideas. Don't be afraid of new solutions, but make sure they fit the needs of your project and your community. At the same time, trust your instincts. In every case, strive for the best. (Chapter 4 presents tips on selecting the best designer possible.)

Be careful about changing the rules in the middle of the game

Establish your ground rules carefully. Take care before you define your proposal or plan of action. Avoid having to change the rules midway in your project. Events do change. Politics, policies, economics, or people may force a drastic revision of your plan. If that situation occurs, take a stark account of your change of focus, ground rules, expectations, and budget, and then plan accordingly. Be extremely clear about future expectations and get agreement in writing about changes made.

Set a realistic budget, work plan, and timetable

Nothing can short-circuit success more quickly than an unrealistic budget, an overly ambitious program with limited resources, or an ill-prepared work plan and timetable. Don't prepare these essential items in a vacuum. Get agreement and clarity before the program is under way. Make sure the client and the design team agree that the work can continue within given guidelines. Continually monitor the progress of the work, the budget, and other constraints. The client has the initial responsibility to set these parameters, but once the client and the design team agree on these factors, it is unfair to complain about problems due to conditions agreed upon earlier. One of the biggest difficulties for designers is persuading their client to set a realistic budget initially and not to ask for the moon with limited resources. Clients, on the other hand, are annoyed when designers groan halfway through the project that they are losing their shirt because they underestimated how much time it would take to complete the work.

Involve the people early on who are affected by (or can affect) your project

Yes, it does take longer to complete a project when you give proper attention to citizen participation and include the people affected by your development. And yes, it is much harder to make decisions when you have more than one person involved. If you ignore this crucial step, however, you will definitely pay for it in the long run. People who feel excluded from the process may find inventive ways to stall or abort your efforts. On a more positive note, involving relevant groups in your process will result in a stronger outcome and will generate a wider network of people dedicated to your project. (Plus, you might learn something and broaden your own point of view.) Solicit new ideas early, before you are on a single-minded track and it is difficult to make changes. Establish early contact with the relevant regulatory agencies, such as those concerned with zoning, environmental impact, historic review, design review, and so forth. If you are not aware of their requirements in the beginning, you will find yourself with unnecessary and costly delays later.

Remember the ultimate user

Who is the main beneficiary of your project? Who is the real client? Who is the main user? The main client is not always the person or organization paying the bill. Although the client for a shopping mall may be the developers, for example, they are not the ultimate user. A state or local public housing authority may fund a development, but the real users are the tenants. Designers, developers, and public officials should consider the people who will ultimately use, enjoy, and benefit from the project. Every detail, every decision should be based on that fact. The life span of development projects exceeds our own. We should consider not only our egocentric needs but the needs of the next generation as well.

Incentives for Change

What causes people to take a stand or take a risk? What encourages them to question the status quo or chart a new direction? One effective ¬motivation is enlightened self-interest. Knowing that altering your course will produce a better product, increase profits, or increase your standing within your network of colleagues, organization, or community is extremely effective. Other people are inspired by more altruistic motives, such as improving the quality of their immediate neighborhood, their environment, or their children's future. In addition to enlightened self-interest or altruistic motives, others find guilt and/or obligation to be powerful mechanisms for change. An incentive based on obligation or guilt may work in the short run, but it is usually not successful in the long term.

The most productive participation occurs when people share certain goals or values and a commitment to the process and outcome of the endeavor. Such incentives for change that are *internally* imposed are most successful. Joint projects initiated with these characteristics are most likely to thrive and continue.

External forces can be a spur for action, most typically through financial or regulatory procedures. You may be required to follow certain guidelines in order to obtain environmental or historic review approval of your development project, for example. Another externally imposed incentive for design change might be the opportunity for increased financial returns by adding public amenities to a project. These incentives or regulations can have a broad impact on our public environment, but they are often complicated to define and enforce.

Effective Roles for Action

Since the process of design and improving our public environment is extremely complex, numerous types of players are involved. Advocates can play a variety of roles as incentives for better design. The most typical players encountered (or the roles you may choose to play) include the following: catalyst, broker/matchmaker/talent scout, educator or technical advisor, partner, leader, participant or implementor, regulator, and reporter or critic. You may have other roles which you could add to this list. In any particular stage of a project, one role may take importance over the others. It is impossible to say, however, which role is most critical overall.

Advocates may, in fact, take on different roles at various stages in the effort, or they may switch roles with the numerous partners in the design and development process. As a citizen concerned about your neighborhood's future, for example, you may first work as a catalyst for change, spurring to action others in more powerful positions. As your expertise grows, you may become the educator of others or the broker/talent scout as you identify opportunities for people or organizations to work on a critical issue. Several pivotal roles for design advocates are described below:

Catalyst

The *catalyst* is a spur to action and is the person who instigates an idea or project, gets people going, and then moves on. This role generates the germ of the idea and inspires others to action. The time frame for this role can be quick and its input meaningful, but implementation of the idea or project is left to others.

Broker/Matchmaker

The *broker/matchmaker/talent scout* identifies opportunities, players, and resources, matching up the resources of one organization with the needs of another. This role differs from the catalyst since it is not a generator of new ideas or initiatives. The broker/matchmaker/talent scout may be asked to take on this function by others. A successful broker matches organizations and individuals who share common concerns or sensitivities but do not typically share the same arena. This partnership is then able to involve an even wider sphere of influence.

Educator

The *educator* or *technical advisor* provides the information, technical knowledge, and expertise necessary to understand the issues and to correctly formulate an approach to a problem. The educator provides a way of thinking about an issue, analyzing it, and presenting information cogently and rationally, and may also offer examples of successful precedents. Ideally the educator should spark discussion and creative thinking to inspire others to action. For the types of design advocacy described in this book, the educator's forum most typically occurs outside an academic setting.

Partners

Partners in design advocacy may evolve after the catalyst initiates action or as a result of two individuals or organizations realizing they share mutually beneficial goals and deciding to work together. Partnerships also evolve when one entity identifies an opportunity, seeks a partner, or relies on an informal broker or matchmaker to establish the relationship. Partners ideally share common values and have a clear understanding of the division of their respective strengths, weaknesses, resources, and responsibilities in the shared endeavor. The time frame and work plan should be developed collaboratively.

Leader

The *leader* in design advocacy creates an idea, a momentum, an enthusiasm, and manages the process or product (or both). The leader may be an organization that affects many entities involved in the design and development process or an individual such as a mayor or chief elected public official. The leader could also be a patron or entrepreneur who is a visionary and can mobilize people and resources.

Participant

The *participant* or *implementor* is the major underpinning or foundation for action. Participants carry out the process, question the approach, hopefully improve upon decisions made, and generally carry the plan to completion. Participants in design advocacy range from those inspired by an unusual action in their own communities (who have little or no experience in design, planning, or activism) to "career" advocates in the design or planning world, who are knowledgeable about the issues and write or speak extensively on the subject. You can't always predict whether a career advocate will be more effective than someone new to the process yet inspired by an unusually compelling issue.

Regulator

The *regulator* controls a set of actions and procedures that influence the built environment. The regulator understands the impact of laws and requirements. Regulations are perceived and used as power, inhibitors, and/or facilitators, depending on their administration and justice. Some regulators use their authority fairly and exert a positive influence on the built environment; others are a major source of frustration when they apply regulations inconsistently and delay results indefinitely. Occasionally regulators take rules meant initially for one purpose and apply them in larger scale ways to influence development. (Environmental regulations are often viewed this way.)

Reporter

The *reporter* or *critic* is able to spark discussion, controversy, agreement, and debate. The role of the reporter or critic is to present information; inform the public; analyze people, places, or events; and, in the critic's role, give opinions and judgments. This role is extremely important in mobilizing people to understand and then to act. Many reporters or critics, however, would argue that their role is *not* one of an advocate. Often a reporter or critic's role becomes one of public education by default when others do not take on that responsibility.

Which of these roles fit your experience or orientation? Can you think of partners, collaborators, or individuals who can be persuaded to adapt their role to accomplish your goals? How do you find these people? Where should you begin—and how do you keep up the momentum? The following chapters will provide answers to difficult questions, examples for inspiration, and tips to help you in your quest.

Chapter 2

CONVINCING ARGUMENTS FOR DESIGN

Doubts and Difficulties

One of the most difficult aspects of design advocacy, particularly in the public sector, is working with public officials who argue against certain expenditures when they are fighting desperately for budgets for police, fire fighters, or the school system. Design is often considered "the icing on the cake," "just aesthetics," or "the responsibility of architects, not public leaders." The truth, of course, is that well-designed neighborhoods and public spaces offer important civic, social, and economic benefits. Public leaders have a pivotal role in this process.

This chapter presents perceptions and arguments you will face in working toward better design of communities, and it will give you answers. The most typical—and often most frustrating—perceptions about design are tackled. Convincing answers are offered to these difficult arguments:

- "Design is only a frill."
- "Design costs too much."
- "Cities shouldn't be concerned about design when we're already struggling with more pressing needs for schools, police and fire departments."

- "Public officials shouldn't worry about design; let's leave that to the designers; I don't know anything about aesthetics."

Responding to Tough Perceptions

There *are* solid responses and examples to use when the only response to your design advocacy is "It costs too much!" This voice of experience comes from people who occupy the seat of power in communities, who juggle impossible budgets every day, and who recognize what works and what doesn't.

To get the answers needed for these difficult questions, I surveyed mayors around the country who participated in the Mayors Institute on City Design sponsored by the National Endowment for the Arts to help mayors understand the significant role they play in design of their communities. In addition, I surveyed experienced professionals who are graduates of the Loeb Fellowship in Advanced Environmental Studies from Harvard University. These people are leaders in design and related professions. They have worked in the trenches and at the top of their organizations and offer their expertise for your use.

Some property owners and developers, the ones who will benefit most directly from design excellence, fail to recognize the connection between quality design and the identity and success of downtown.
    MAYOR BILL HARRIS, LINCOLN, NEBRASKA

The level of awareness and concern among city staff about design issues needs to be raised. They must understand that the sooner design issues are questioned in a project, the easier it is to make the necessary changes. It is equally important to educate the public

*about the importance of good design in public projects and the need
to maintain the public environment.*
MAYOR THOMAS P. RYAN, JR., ROCHESTER, NEW YORK

Mayors eternally struggle with municipal budget battles
and hear the loudest complaints about expenditures of public
dollars. The mayors surveyed quickly identified the frustrating
and widespread dilemma of juggling competing demands for
limited public resources. Many mentioned a lack of understanding by staff and citizens about design quality and its
impact on their community. They also cited a struggle between
the need to fill potholes while at the same time creating a vision
for the future of their city.

This chapter will cite the mayors' concerns head-on and
provide you with some answers from the experts themselves.
Let's address the most difficult perceptions and questions first,
the ones you hear most often.

"Design is only a frill"

Too often people view design as unimportant, an afterthought,
or something to be worried about by others. This mind-set is
particularly troublesome when shared by people in power who
make important decisions affecting you and your quality of
life. Not all people understand that design is integral not only
to the look of a product or place, but also to its use, long-term
viability, and enjoyment. Whether you are considering your
coffee cup, your office, your home, or your city streets, design
is basic to the ultimate test. Does this product or place work for
you? Does it meet your needs?

Here are some valid responses to the assertion "Design is
only a frill":

"So are the clothes we wear," asserts Mayor Sue Myrick of
Charlotte, North Carolina, "but they say something about who
we are, and they have an impression on what people think of
us. In like manner, well-designed cities are a reflection of its
people and its government and leave lasting impressions on its
citizens and visitors."

Mayor Charles Farmer of Jackson, Tennessee, defines
design using character-building terms and concern about the

future: "Unlike frills—here today and gone tomorrow—design is a long-range plan to which we have the obligation to protect the 'not yet born' whose lives will be shaped by so-called frills. Unlike a frill, good civic design creates character, vitality, and a sense of place."

GOOD DESIGN MAKES A CITY WORK BETTER,
NOT JUST LOOK BETTER.

"Challenge anyone to name his or her favorite place and then ask why," argues Mayor John Bullard of New Bedford, Massachusetts. "Many of the reasons that attractive places are attractive have to do with design. Without these design elements, a specific place becomes just anywhere. Design of a city communicates what it is. It is as much a frill as your face is."

Design a frill? Design relates directly to economic development and equals cold hard cash for many communities. The planning, design, and overall character of a city can be the deciding factor on a major corporation or employer locating in your community or the one next door. According to Mayor Michael Polovitz of Grand Forks, North Dakota, "Design reflects on the city as a whole. How a city looks to new business is very important to whether or not that business locates in your city."

Design relates directly to an impression of livability and economic vitality. It has a major impact on our city.
    MAYOR DAVID MUSANTE, JR., NORTHAMPTON, MASSACHUSETTS

This decision means increased jobs, a broader tax base, and a stronger economic base for your community. Well-designed buildings and neighborhoods encourage increased property values that tie directly into municipal coffers. Efficient and well-designed roadways, public transportation systems, and residential environments enable workers to live and work in the same community, for example, as opposed to placing undue municipal burdens on one town while employees' tax dollars go to another.

Increased product value from quality design is readily apparent. Just consider automobiles or clothing. The same results are found in good city design. Listen to these experts:

In the private sector, well-designed products will succeed in tight markets where poorly designed products will not. We have demonstrated this time and time again in master-planned communities which simply out perform the marketplace either through higher absorption rates, greater market shares, higher prices, and so forth. Better designed projects are better mousetraps.
    MICHAEL HORST, PBR, SAN FRANCISCO, CALIFORNIA

Design is critical to the marketability of any commercial property, especially in the kind of real estate market downturn we are experiencing now in New England. Good design may in fact make property somewhat recession-proof.
    ELEANOR WHITE, MASSACHUSETTS HOUSING FINANCE AUTHORITY, BOSTON, MASSACHUSETTS

Most people don't notice good design, but subconsciously, they do *feel bad [design] or non design. Design is* the *most important ingredient in making our environment better.*
    RONALD M. DRUKER, THE DRUKER COMPANY, BOSTON, MASSACHUSETTS

Our view of design and the public good is evolving. Over time, we are realizing the increasing value and responsibility of designers and planners in design of the public environment. This change is most notable with public housing. Consider this perspective:

Design is the difference whether it works well or not. If that's a frill . . . Many public housing projects were built with very little investment in design, since (the thought was) the poor don't deserve it. What were the savings? What has been—and will continue to be— the costs in both economic and quality of life terms? We are paying a very *big price in public housing alone.*
    MARY MEANS, MEANS AND ASSOCIATES, ALEXANDRIA, VIRGINIA

You've heard some convincing arguments about the importance of design. But how can you convince the powers-that-be to pay for it? How can you respond to the next common argument.

"Design costs too much"

This argument is the one you'll hear the loudest. Concurrent with the view "Design is a frill," many people just don't understand the financial implications and benefits of good design. They equate "design" with expensive marble and gold leaf trim. A better understanding would acknowledge design as essential decisions of use, form, content, and relationships with surrounding places and people. The refrain should not be "Design costs too much" but rather "*Bad* design costs too much."

Mayors probably hear this cost complaint as much as anyone. Here are their responses:

I'm more concerned about bad designs wasting public or private investment than I am about excellent design adding a few dollars to the cost of a project.
MAYOR JOSEPH S. DADDONA, ALLENTOWN, PENNSYLVANIA

It is imperative that those people making decisions on design today must look ahead 30 to 40 years, because the decisions made today will be a part of our community and affect design for many years.
MAYOR JACK WHITE, SIOUX FALLS, SOUTH DAKOTA

Good design is not necessarily more expensive. Materials cost the same whether the design is good or bad.
MAYOR JOHN HODGES, WILLIAMSBURG, VIRGINIA

My experience has been that people soon forget how much a project costs. However, the quality of a project, or the lack of it, affects people for decades.
MAYOR JOHN BULLARD, NEW BEDFORD, MASSACHUSETTS

Now let's hear from the design and development community, who are concerned with the bottom line as well as the look of a project:

Excellent design is not the same as elaborate or expensive design (although it may be in some cases); some excellent design may in fact compensate for smaller square feet and less expensive materials. A poorly designed project cuts the chance of success and increases the risk. It is very expensive to go back and correct design problems later.
ELEANOR WHITE, MASSACHUSETTS HOUSING FINANCE AGENCY,
BOSTON, MASSACHUSETTS

Cost is only one part of the financial analysis equation. The complete equation is revenues minus costs equals returns. If increased costs can be offset by increased revenues, profits will be at least as

much. Moreover, returns can be nonfinancial so that public benefits could be included in the equation as well.
     MICHAEL HORST, PBR, SAN FRANCISCO, CALIFORNIA

Design decisions and allocations of financial resources are not made unilaterally. To be an effective advocate for quality design, we must convince others of its value. This task is particularly difficult when public dollars are shrinking dramatically, social and economic problems are increasing, and battles for resources are more intense. In this environment, the following argument becomes even more difficult to answer.

"Design is not important compared to our shrinking public dollars for schools, police, and fire departments"

This argument is one of the most difficult to answer. With public funds becoming even more scarce, it is difficult to argue for design. One answer is that we are not arguing for *design*, per se. We are arguing to make our cities work better to fit our needs, to be more efficient, more accessible, easier to navigate, safer, and more desirable places in which to live. Here are responses from mayors, controllers of the public purse strings, to that difficult dilemma:

Many problems that we are experiencing in our urban centers stem from people's frustration with their surrounding environment. The ability of most cities to fund the educational, public safety, and public works services that control that environment is dependent upon the level of private investment and development that supports their local tax base. Good design policies certainly have a positive impact on that level of investment and development.
     MAYOR THOMAS P. RYAN, JR., ROCHESTER, NEW YORK

Good design attracts people to a city, and those people help pay for essentials that help instill pride and satisfaction in what citizens get for their taxes. Poor design contributes to the decline of property values, of the tax base, and of resources available for essential services.
     MAYOR BILL HARRIS, LINCOLN, NEBRASKA

Design is an important element of necessary municipal services. By making the environment more comfortable and conducive to learning, our children learn better. Design is especially important in

*our public safety areas where state-of-the-art facilities and equip-
ment enhance response time and police and fire effectiveness.*
    MAYOR SHARP JAMES, NEWARK, NEW JERSEY

Designers and developers who work in the public realm
have equally persuasive arguments to offer:

*This discussion is really one of capital versus operating costs. Work
through particular examples of well-designed schools versus poorly
designed ones, well-designed sewage treatment plants versus poorly
designed ones, Chernobyl versus self-correcting reactors, the San
Diego County Jail where inmates escape by punching holes through
the wall because they reduced the budget, bridges that collapse
versus ones that don't.*
    GENE SLATER, CAINE GRESSEL MIDLEY SLATER, SAN FRANCISCO,
    CALIFORNIA

*The relative cost of design is pennies and can save or leverage
millions.*
    MARY MEANS, MEANS AND ASSOCIATES, ALEXANDRIA, VIRGINIA

*Design and planning, or lack of it, can make or break a city. Port-
land's downtown has been saved because of planning and good
design . . . Without the planning and design, the center of the city
would have been deserted years ago.*
    MAYOR BUD CLARK, PORTLAND, OREGON

*When we build public facilities that look like prisons, people re-
spond and act like outlaws. Good design generates respect on the
part of the public and care by maintenance personnel. Design is a
critical component in any project.*
    KENNETH KRUCKEMEYER, FORMER ASSOCIATE COMMISSIONER,
    MASSACHUSETTS DEPARTMENT OF PUBLIC WORKS

You now have heard convincing arguments about design
not just being a "frill," costing too much, or not meriting public
investment. Often the most difficult obstacle to design advocacy, however, is making public officials aware of their power
and influence over the future of your community. Leadership
and awareness at the top are most important because their
impact filters down to every level in a community.

Advocates for quality design insist on attention to this issue
by top leadership. Time and time again, state and local agency
employees complain that if only they could get their bosses to
understand the importance of design on a particular project,

their job would be so much easier. Design advocacy is more effective when power brokers and decision makers capitalize on their leadership positions. Nevertheless, you constantly hear the following argument.

"Public officials shouldn't worry about design; let's leave that to the designers; I don't know anything about aesthetics"
Here are some convincing responses to those statements from the mayors themselves:

No official has more power over design than a mayor. And power over design is what we are talking about. It is easier to educate mayors about design than it is to give power to designers.
MAYOR JOHN BULLARD, NEW BEDFORD, MASSACHUSETTS

As city officials, we have different interests than architects or developers. We have to be concerned about the cumulative effect of design decisions while architects or developers often are only concerned about one particular design.
MAYOR THOMAS P. RYAN, JR., ROCHESTER, NEW YORK

Individual designers are concerned only with their particular project and their clients' needs. It is the responsibility of public officials to concern themselves with the relationship of different projects to the context of the city.
MAYOR SUE MYRICK, CHARLOTTE, NORTH CAROLINA

Design sets a city's image, both to visitors and to residents . . . Mayors who think they are not involved in design in the downtown areas just aren't doing the whole job.
MAYOR BILL HARRIS, LINCOLN, NEBRASKA

All mayors should be concerned with the aesthetic effect of their city on both visitors and residents. Design is the first thing you see and the last thing you remember.
MAYOR DAVID ARMSTRONG, NATCHEZ, MISSISSIPPI

Lessons from Success

You have just heard the most recurring complaints or excuses about design, along with convincing arguments and answers from experts in the field. As an advocate of quality design, you can learn from examples where difficult problems were solved, heated controversies settled, and citizens, designers, and public officials worked successfully to make a difference.

These examples are drawn from the survey given to alumni of Harvard University's Loeb Fellowship in Advanced Environmental Studies who are national experts in design, planning, and public development. In each of the examples identified through this survey, factors pivotal to quality design are identified. The issues and frustrations described may sound hauntingly familiar. Perhaps the solutions or strategies used to solve these difficult examples could be adapted to help your own effort to improve your community.

The examples presented here are just a few of countless successful design advocacy struggles found annually around the country. The purpose of these quick sketches is to demonstrate the range and variety of effective design advocacy strategies. By learning that others shared many of your own obstacles and difficulties and found a solution, you may find inspiration and tips for your own efforts.

The impact of commercial development along highways, for example, can devastate communities if such development is not well planned. Citizens in Birmingham, Alabama, took an aggressive lead. A private nonprofit group called the Horizon 280 Association was created to monitor development standards for the twelve miles of highway along U.S. 280 leading through the Birmingham metropolitan area. According to Philip A. Morris, executive editor of *Southern Living* of Birmingham, Alabama, the factors that led to the success of this initiative included:

- A clearly identified choice between strip commercial and a more attractive approach to development at a key point, just before rapid development began
- Association Board balanced between major landowners/developers and the public sector
- Monthly breakfast meetings that provided good contacts for a variety of purposes
- Major landowners with vision to do good planning on their own land who set an example
- Annual awards program that highlighted both good and bad development in the area

The successful outcome took extensive work. According to Morris, "the initial organization and definition was not easy.

You must get the group to identify the problem, even if you already know it. The key problem of the Horizon 280 Association was the difficulty of turning business types into a politically astute group. They want to give orders (most are CEO's), not request and influence action."

Quality of affordable housing is another challenging example faced by every community. Requiring good design by a public agency is a bold and sometimes difficult task. The Massachusetts Housing Finance Agency (MHFA) created the SHARP program that produced approximately 10,000 housing units from 1984 to 1990. According to Eleanor White of MHFA, quality design was mandated by "building it into the competitive scoring system from the outset, to assure that any projects receiving funding would be well designed (with more scoring points given to the best design)." Factors leading to the success of this program included:

- Absolute adherence by MHFA to a very high threshold standard of acceptability.
- The attractiveness of the financing program to developers created a major incentive to maximize scoring points.
- The need to market completed units to 75% nonsubsidized tenants created a market discipline and perceived real-world need to have good design.

These first two factors could be replicated for virtually any public program that provides an economic incentive to the applicant. The golden rule was also cited by White, "He who has the gold sets the rules."

Convincing applicants to this program that the state was serious about quality design was not easy at first. As noted by White, "Initially, many examples of poor design were submitted. It took the courageous step of failing a proposal for design reasons for the point to be made to the applicant community that MHFA was serious about this issue. MHFA also provided a great deal of technical assistance to prospective applicants so that the best possible design was encouraged."

Often a need for technical assistance and comprehension of basic design issues offer an unparalleled opportunity for design advocacy and education. In the early days of the National Trust for Historic Preservation, staff traveled around the country providing technical assistance to communities. The National Trust identified substantial need for smaller cities and towns to save

downtown buildings and reclaim their urban vitality. They all seemed to "either be doing bootstraps and bandaids or to be copying big city 'solutions' that were wildly out of scale with their problems," according to Mary Means of Means and Associates in Alexandria, Virginia. In an entrepreneurial spirit, a laboratory demonstration project developed "practical and workable strategies for preservation-based downtown development—it became known as the Main Street approach."[2] Means noted that the success factors for this program included:

- Timing, circumstances . . . funding source
- Admitting that we had no idea what would work, but we wanted to work in collaboration with real towns to find real solutions that could help them and others. . . .Making them *owners,* too
- Choosing excellent staff, highly motivated and high energy . . . then instilling a sense of team work among them
- Instinctively building bridges and partnerships at the local level with other allied organizations who could help
- Building ownership in the solutions by involving the potential actors in their design and planning
- Documenting it all from base level all the way through— otherwise there's no tangible way to show the effect
- Communication and promotion

    Intensive citizen involvement is the hallmark of another example of successful advocacy by Chattanooga Venture's "Vision 2000." This initiative is an extension of the public participation and focus groups held in 1984 which led to the creation of the Tennessee River Master Plan. Chattanooga Venture, created as an outgrowth of that process, helped chart a new course for the city in an era of high unemployment and serious tensions in the community. Their efforts resulted in significant, long-term benefits for Chattanooga. A nonprofit River City Company oversaw the redevelopment of the downtown area and the river front. A citizen task force raised funds to create a Family Violence Shelter. Local citizens raised funds for renovation of the historic Tivoli Theater. The deteriorating Walnut Street Bridge was restored, along with a linear park and other greenways along the river. Other major capital projects such as the Tennessee Aquarium and the Metropolitan Airport were completed.

Underlying these tangible projects is an essential foundation of communication and broad-based involvement. According to one community volunteer, LaFonde McGee:

Vision 2000 broke down barriers . . . We had a very divided city— divided by class, race, history and geography. We had a mindset about the power structure, about who's powerful and who's powerless in this community. And it was so dominant in our thinking that we were paralyzed from action. So when we were all invited to the table to participate in creating a new vision for the city, we looked around and we saw so many people and such diversity that it broke down the myth of how things get done. Since [Vision 2000], we have had experiences working together that help us understand each others' cultures better.[3]

Chattanooga Venture revisited the goals that were identified through this process in 1993 through "ReVision 2000." Participation was even greater than in the earlier process, with 2,600 people actively involved. Specific goals were identified, reflecting key issues such as economic development, downtown improvement, parenting and the family, parks and greenways, the environment, housing, government, and culture and the arts. The community, business, and government are now working to implement specific recommendations.

Citizen input and long-term involvement were also crucial for the final example, the Southwest Corridor Project in Boston. This project involved renewal of a series of Boston neighborhoods along a corridor originally cleared for an interstate highway through the construction of a new rapid transit and railroad line, local streets, park land, and public and private development. Factors that led to the success of this long-term, complicated project, as identified by respondents to the Loeb survey, included:

- An involved citizenry
- A small, aggressive project management team with authority (gubernatorial appointment) and independence

- Financial commitment at the federal and state levels
- Organizing adjacent residents and keeping them as positive participants in project design and environmental review stages . . . Also persistence—fifteen years of it
- Project managers who were determined, not bureaucratic, who were responsive and had taste
- A consistent quality of design details, a good finish
- Well-designed bridges and highways which integrate the landscape into them
- Stations which respond to a sense of place[4]

The change of political power threatened the project at state and local levels, according to Kenneth Kruckemeyer, former associate commissioner of the Massachusetts Department of Public Works, "but an involved citizenry kept the project true to the mark . . . Without a strong set of goals, it is easy to fall prey to the trap of compromise in order 'to get things built'."

Cutting costs is always a hazard. Your project will be a rare one, indeed, if a carving knife is not poised precariously close to shave costs at every turn. As one developer and former public official described the process with the Southwest Corridor project:

There is always someone with a knife who is absolutely sure he can do it cheaper. Someone in authority has to say 'We're not going to do it the old way.' It is important to get the project in the public eye. Someone will also see the problems, particularly if you are dealing with people who are genuine. Another way is to educate people by example. Show what works and what doesn't . . . It is good insurance to have public input. In the end, with the Southwest Corridor Project, it was our colleagues in government who tried to cut back. With so much public momentum built up for support, we were able to keep in what the citizens wanted.

TONY PANGARO, FORMER DEVELOPMENT COORDINATOR OF SOUTHWEST CORRIDOR PROJECT

This project symbolizes an extraordinarily complex undertaking with many players, conflicting agendas, ambitious goals, and a successful outcome. Not every public project need be so complicated, costly, and lengthy to produce a successful outcome.

One important ingredient to success of a public project is to carefully *listen* to the concerns of citizens, public officials, and participants in the design and development process. *Re-*

sponding to these concerns in a reasonable, timely, fair, and creative manner will move the project along faster than you realize. Finally, a sense of humor is an essential trait that is often overlooked in the complex and often frustrating process of public development.

The argument that good design can not occur in the public realm will be made loudly, forcefully, and often. The lessons learned from design advocates, mayors, and experts in the field provide evidence to the contrary. Hopefully the answers to the arguments presented in this chapter and the lessons learned from successful projects will help you in your work.

Chapter 3

TARGETING PUBLIC WORKS AND TRANSPORTATION

Contrary to public perception, public agencies offer an important opportunity for innovation and testing of new design ideas on a large scale. Where else can you find a legislatively defined mandate, a budget created solely for public improvements, and an experienced work force in place? Without prodding, public agencies may not always recognize this opportunity or be willing to exercise it, but the design advocate can identify willing leadership and opportunities too beneficial for the agency to be rejected. Most importantly, these ideas frequently can be implemented without undue additional expenditures of public funds.

WITH THE RIGHT LEADERSHIP, PUBLIC AGENCIES OFFER A CHANCE FOR INNOVATION AND A HUGE IMPACT. WHERE ELSE CAN A GOOD IDEA BENEFIT AN ENTIRE CITY OR STATE?

Which techniques work the best? Creating new partnerships or collaborations, working to educate and inspire agency staff, testing new ideas, and providing successful examples are the best places to begin. Often the very fact that a new collaboration or pilot project is taking place will serve as an incentive for people to innovate, as opposed to using the familiar approach that "we always use here." Nothing gives people a better idea of the way things *could* be done than a successful example. The pilot program doesn't necessarily have to test a

33

ground-breaking new idea. The very act of initiating a program indicates to others that the agency places an emphasis on design and cares about the outcome.

One of the most effective opportunities for design advocacy is working with public agencies who have the mandate and the resources for construction and development. Transportation and public works departments on a state and local level, for example, spend millions of dollars annually on road, highway, and bridge construction in communities. Their construction requirements are carefully regulated by federal and state legislation, as well as by agency guidelines and standards. Although public agencies pay scrupulous attention to these requirements, they do not always consider the design impact of these huge investments on neighborhoods or the natural environment. The potential for making a difference on a large scale led the Massachusetts Council on the Arts and Humanities to begin establishing pilot projects on design.

An Unusual Partnership in Bridge Design

In the earliest stages of the Design and Development Program, the Executive Director of the Council, Anne Hawley, and the Deputy Commissioner of the state's Division of Capital Planning and Operations, Tunney Lee, met with the Commissioner of the Massachusetts Department of Public Works, Robert Tierney, to scout out possible pilot projects. Since a major goal of the Council's emerging design program was creation of pilot projects with other state agencies, they asked Commissioner Tierney if he could suggest any areas of possible collaboration. He noted that the Commonwealth renovated or constructed over one hundred bridges each year and suggested that bridge design might be a fruitful area for a partnership. The purpose of this collaboration was to highlight the importance of quality bridge design and to emphasize its relationship to developing technologies and superior construction.

"DESIGN?" THE HEAD ENGINEER RESPONDED.
"YES, WE USED TO HAVE ONE ARCHITECT IN OUR DEPARTMENT. HIS JOB WAS TO CHOOSE THE LOCATION FOR THE STATE SEAL ON THE BRIDGES AFTER WE FINISHED BUILDING THEM."

The Massachusetts Department of Public Works was typical of many state public works departments. In the 1940s and '50s, the Department employed approximately 5,000 people, and of that number, only one was a bridge architect. The perception of the architect's role was that "he was the one that prettied up the bridges after the engineers finished with them." No other role for architects was envisioned other than designing facades of stonework to make the concrete abutments of the bridges look as if they were old.

State public works departments adhere religiously to the *Bridge Manual* that details federal requirements for bridge design from the Federal Highway Administration. If you looked up the word *design* in this lengthy document, you saw only the briefest of references such as the following:

The Design Criteria shall be stated relative to the following:

a. *The number of lanes, width of shoulder and provisions for sidewalks.*
b. *Vertical and horizontal alignment of highways.*
c. *Vertical and horizontal clearances.*
d. *Design loading for the structure.*
e. *Safety features.*

Nowhere in the manual would you see a discussion of the overall impact and relationship of the bridge design to the connecting roadways, landscape, and adjacent community.

To change this situation, the Massachusetts Council on the Arts and Humanities and the Massachusetts Department of Public Works decided to educate the engineers responsible for designing the state's bridges. The Department typically would issue contracts for engineering consultants to design the state bridges. To put the scale of design and construction of bridges in perspective, a typical 100-foot steel bridge required up to $200,000 in design fees (including environmental and other required reviews) and $1,000,000 in total construction costs over a *thirteen* year period. The Department of Public Works' cost in overseeing the project to manage the process and provide a site office with inspectors would typically add 30% to the cost of construction, or $300,000 for this prototypical bridge, thus increasing the total costs to $1,500,000. The lengthy period for construction of the bridge is attributed to the required local, state, and federal reviews, the state public bidding requirements requiring a complete and separate set of construction documents, and the management process used in the department.[5]

This bridge design program was perhaps the most productive and unusual partnership of all the Council endeavors. Although a partnership of bridge technology and design seemed extremely logical to our two agencies, people were constantly asking us, "How did the state *arts* council and the state *public works* department ever get together?" The two agencies learned and benefited from each other every step of the way. The program was able to expose engineers and designers of state bridges to the newest in bridge design technologies and aesthetics. The staff and consultants of the Massachusetts Department of Public Works learned much about the profession of bridge design: who is involved in all the facets of the process and the implications of bridge design to their efforts. Finally, the staff of the department was energized in its task. The technical training made them think more about their professional responsibility and the need to know more about contemporary technology and become involved in bridge design nationwide.

The Council learned how it could function effectively as a catalyst in working with other state agencies to further design quality and education. Other states and localities emulated the bridge design program. This pilot project also served as an example for additional Council design programs described in subsequent chapters of this book.

The partnership[6] resulted in a major conference and series of technical workshops entitled "Bridge Design: Aesthetics and Developing Technologies." The conference proceedings evolved into a book of the same title that was distributed nationally. The conference, funded by the National Endowment for the Arts and the two state agencies, was extremely well received by the participants. This enthusiasm stemmed in part from the fact that long-term public employees are rarely recognized for the quality of their work or for their commitment to their work. A major premise of the bridge design conference was that public employees *want* to be exposed to new ideas and to expand their professional knowledge. Many of the consulting engineers who participated in the workshops expressed frank surprise that the state would sponsor such an extensive educational program. The bridge design conference and resulting publication helped dispel prejudices that government does not strive for excellence. As one engineer commented:

Your conference showed us that the Department of Public Works has higher standards for design excellence and expects its staff and consultants to share those expectations, as well.

Not only did the conference format expect participants to listen and learn, but it gave them a chance to share their own experiences and ideas. At one of the most intriguing sessions, participants were divided into small working groups and asked to draw their own ideas on bridge design. The resulting illustrations were shared with the department staff and leadership and included in the conference proceedings that was distributed throughout the country.

One surprising aspect of planning this conference was the difficulty in identifying national leaders in bridge design. In contrast to the architectural profession, which sponsors numerous publications and awards ceremonies and is featured daily in the public press, engineers are not well known or publicized. With extensive research and questioning, we uncovered a cross section of the best national talent for the conference. They gave presentations on the following topics:

- *Aesthetics—The Challenge,* evaluating various methods of arriving at bridge designs, including design competitions
- *The Role of the Public Agency,* reviewing development attitudes and examples of public bridge design
- *The Bridge in Context,* presenting the Boston Southwest Corridor Project's 22 bridges as a case study
- *The Consultant's Role,* providing guidance in the bridge type selection, structure proportions, and latest technology

Three subsequent workshops expanded on information presented at the main conference:

- *Bridge Type Studies,* which evaluated the various stages of bridge type development
- *Bridge Details,* such as screening, fences, railings, color, texture, and landscape treatment, which can enhance or destroy the design of a bridge
- *Developing Technologies,* focusing on concrete and steel construction and their impact on aesthetics

The response to the conference and related workshops was overwhelming. In our planning, we anticipated approximately 150 to 200 people would attend the conference and 50 people would attend each workshop. Instead, over 400 people registered for and attended the conference, and 200 people participated in each of the three technical workshops. The director of one state agency noted that when she arrived at the conference, "I thought people were lined up to buy tickets to a rock concert, not attend a conference on bridge design."

To augment the learning that occurred during the conference series, we mounted two exhibitions on bridge design at the adjacent State Transportation Building. One highlighted bridges of the famous Swiss bridge engineer Christian Menn, and the other illustrated award-winning bridges from the California Department of Transportation. Catalogs describing the two exhibits were also included in the appendix to the book on bridge design that was an outgrowth of the conference. These exhibitions generated discussion, debate, and much learning by hundreds of state transportation workers and citizens who passed by the exhibit daily. State transportation workers crowded around the exhibition on their lunch break, pointing out technical feats of the award-winning bridges.

Inspiring people with conferences and good examples is an important strategy for design advocacy. Keeping this momentum going and developing it into commitment and implementation of quality design is even more essential. To this end, an outgrowth of the bridge design conferences was revision of the state's *Bridge Manual* to include serious attention to design. The Massachusetts Department of Public Works entered into a three-year contract with bridge engineer Arvid Grant of Arvid Grant and Associates in Olympia, Washington. He was one of the speakers at the bridge design conference and previously won a Presidential Design Award for his Pasco/Kennewick Intercity Bridge over the Columbia River in Washington. Grant also was engaged to write a guideline to bridge type studies as an introduction to the state's *Bridge Manual.*

The bridge type study is the document prepared during the schematic design stage and establishes the basic character and ultimate success of any bridge design. Through drawings and calculations, the bridge type study analyzes the size and shape of the bridge, determines the type and amount of materials needed, and evaluates a couple of bridge design alternatives. The overview to the *Bridge Manual* providing guidelines to bridge type studies was intended to strengthen the emphasis of design as integrated into the entire engineering and construction process of building bridges.

THE PASCO/KENNEWICK INTERCITY BRIDGE WON A PRESIDENTIAL DESIGN AWARD AND REPRESENTS THE POTENTIAL OF COMBINING BRIDGE AESTHETICS WITH ENGINEERING TECHNOLOGY.

In his conference remarks to the bridge designers of Massachusetts, Grant outlined the criteria for civil engineering work:

> *The work of a civil engineer should meet three criteria. A design should be structurally correct and economically efficient; it should · do the most work with the least material. A structure should also be designed so as never to cause injury—either physical or emotional. An ugly bridge is injurious to the senses. The aesthetic value of a work is, thus, as important as its economic or structural value. To serve the public, the civil engineer must deliver not only economic and structural integrity, but also beauty. For the past fifty years, however, American bridge designers have often neglected to consider aesthetics. Designers, therefore, have been remiss in their task of delivering beauty, and government has been remiss in its role of protecting the public from injury.[7]*

Bridge Design Competition

After the success of the bridge design conference series, the Massachusetts Department of Public Works and the Massachusetts Council on the Arts and Humanities wanted to continue our successful collaboration. To highlight the public's role in striving for design excellence, we decided to sponsor jointly a national bridge design competition. The two agencies jointly applied for and received a Design Arts grant from the National Endowment for the Arts to support this endeavor. We selected a professional advisor to supervise the competition, developed the work plan, and began work in earnest.

The selection of the appropriate site was extremely important. We wanted the bridge site to pose interesting design questions for the competitors, yet at the same time be typical of some of the one hundred other bridges constructed by the Department of Public Works annually. Our hope was that creative solutions evolved from the competition could inform other sites in the state. During our planning process, Christian Menn agreed to participate as a jury member. He won or served as a juror in numerous bridge design competitions in Switzerland and Europe, and we were eager for his advice. (In contrast to the United States, bridge design competitions are a well-established mechanism for eliciting the best in bridge design in other parts of the world.) We sent Menn summaries of the top site alternatives to consider for a national design competition. After reviewing several options, we selected a bridge site over the Merrimac River Valley in Lowell, Massachusetts.

The cosponsors were eager to announce the program nationally. Unfortunately, during the early planning stages it became clear that the site in question had to undergo additional state environmental review approvals since the access road to the bridge was plotted to go through a landfill site and was adjacent to an historic building. The alternative road would have passed through an historic site in the city of Lowell. We were forced to delay the competition for close to a year while the environmental review was completed.

During this time, the state's fiscal situation deteriorated drastically. The Commonwealth issued a temporary ban on the hiring of all consultants, even though the Department of Public Works relied almost completely on consulting engineers to design and build the states' bridges. We did not want to announce the competition until we had 100% assurance that the winning bridge could be constructed. With great reluctance, we halted our plans for the bridge design competition and returned our grant to the National Endowment for the Arts. We were especially disappointed because the United States had not spon-

THE WINNING DESIGN OF THE VERMONT TIMBER BRIDGE DESIGN COMPETITION SERVES AS AN EXAMPLE FOR A HUNDRED WOODEN BRIDGES THROUGHOUT THE STATE. (PHOTOGRAPH BY KENNETH KRUCKEMEYER.)

sored a professional bridge design competition since the competition for the bridge over the Harlem River that occurred in 1889. We were eager to start the momentum again in our country.

Fortunately our neighbors at the Vermont Council on the Arts and the Vermont Agency of Transportation were able to carry on our enthusiasm for bridge design. They jointly sponsored the Vermont Timber Bridge Design Competition, a national competition to design a prototype short-span highway bridge that would be both economically feasible and well designed. The sponsors first held a timber bridge conference in Vermont to present information on the use, construction, and maintenance of timber bridges. Competitors submitted conceptual plans, presentation boards, and engineering specifications. The winning design was a classic kingpost truss bridge praised by the jury as representing the "historic simplicity, industry, and heritage of Vermont." The bridge is expected to serve as a prototype for the future replacement of 100 covered bridges remaining in the state. This collaboration raised the level of debate for quality design in the state, forged a productive partnership between two disparate state agencies, and brought national attention to Vermont's commitment to the quality of its public environment.

A Leap Forward in Highway Landscape Design

A demonstration in highway landscape design was the Massachusetts Council on the Arts and Humanities' earliest pilot project with another state agency. We joined forces with the Massachusetts Turnpike Authority, the agency responsible for construction, operation, and maintenance of the major east-west 135-mile toll highway which crosses the state. Although the Authority has always been extremely diligent about maintenance and operation of the roadways, at that time landscape design was not a major priority.

The chairman of the Authority was asked to identify a location with high visibility in the state which would benefit from design improvements. He recommended a 30-acre site along the interchange in the town of Lee, which served as an entrance to the Berkshire Mountains and western Massachusetts. Over 2.2 million people pass by this prominent location annually, so it was well suited for design improvement. A landscape design professor at the University of Massachusetts in Amherst was asked to develop a conceptual design scheme emphasizing the unique characteristics of the site and the opportunity for environmental art as part of the landscape design scheme. He was also asked to design a plan which could be implemented by existing Turnpike personnel using materials readily at hand and with reasonable cost. The modest design costs of this preliminary plan were divided between the Massachusetts Council on the Arts, the Chancellor of the University, and the Turnpike Authority. Sharing of the costs was an incentive necessary to initiate the project at this early stage.

The designer proposed a creative work of environmental art/landscape design for the site. Although the Authority accepted many of the basic elements, the more far-reaching environmental art aspects of the plan were rejected after extensive debate. Some of the elements of the plan were considered to be safety hazards by the staff engineers, although architects thought otherwise. An additional argument against the design was the concern that the costs of implementation were too high. The Authority anticipated that existing staff could not add this complex project to their current work load, and that they would have to hire contractors to complete the landscaping. After a year of hard work, the project was almost stopped.

Ultimately a staff member at the Authority revised the original landscape plan to a much more basic approach while maintaining some of the earlier elements. Many of the existing problems at the site, such as drainage and soil erosion, were solved through adaptation of the previous designs' site improvements. New landscaping, wild flower plantings, and shrubs and trees were also recommended. The original environmental art components of the design were rejected. These elements included such items as landscape treatments for covering the rather plain toll booths and a series of panels made from fencing components covered by planting in artistic patterns to be added along the highway.

The revised plan earned the approval of MassPike's staff and Board. The Authority decided to use its staff to participate in implementing the new design. Initially the intent was to ask the maintenance staff to help only in the first stages of the project (with subsequent work to be contracted out to other landscapers). The maintenance crew agreed to this new task and found much satisfaction in their work. The Authority personnel took on more and more steps of the construction of the landscape design, reducing the overall costs and bringing pride and reward to their job.

When the project was completed, the Authority personnel took great care to ensure that this large parcel of land was the best maintained of all the Turnpike properties. This project later received a Beautification Award from a landscape design awards program administered by the Governor's Office, and it also serves as testimony to the fact that perseverance does pay off.

A dedicated Board member of the Massachusetts Turnpike Authority, the late Anne McHugh, appraised this project:

This piece of land is the best maintained property along the Turnpike and will continue to be the best maintained property. The workers are proud of their work. It really made a difference. This project will spur the Board on to increased landscaping along the Turnpike.

An important outcome is this state agency reassessing its role as the guardian of the main roadway throughout the state.

In addition to previous and significant roles as the builder, maintainer, and protector of this highway, the Authority now saw its role expanded to improve the public environment for the millions of travelers who cross the state each year. As evident in the following section on public works and art, new leadership in this agency later initiated creative improvements to the public landscape.

Since the completion of this project, further landscape design work was initiated by the Massachusetts Turnpike Authority and other state offices. Today, the Turnpike Authority employs the first permanent professional landscape architect in the history of the agency; this staff member coordinates closely with the engineering and maintenance departments. The new landscape management program incorporates different methods to manage each of the major ecological areas of the Turnpike corridor. These techniques include "thinning strands of trees and woodlands, monitoring wetland complexes, modifying mowing practices, and seeding wild flower meadows."[8]

The prevalence of wild flowers along the Turnpike is the improvement that is perhaps most visible and appreciated by the public. Active participation by the Turnpike in the well-attended Flower Show held in Boston each year is a tangible sign to the public that this public agency takes seriously its mandate to improve the quality of the highway which runs through their state. Participation in the Flower Show is also a creative opportunity for the agency to educate people about their approach to active management of the roadside.

Close involvement and communication among the landscape, maintenance, and engineering crews continue to be key factors in the success of new programs proposed by the Authority. This participation is essential in any effort which attempts to change old rules and procedures. Such interaction should not simply be limited to projects related to public works, since involving people who implement the new ideas is critical for the success of any innovative endeavor.

Public Works and Art

A trip to Maryland by the Vice-Chairwoman of the Massachusetts Turnpike Authority, Ann Hershfang, may change forever the way the agency paints its bridges. She was struck by the un-

THE PAINT DESIGN OF THIS BRIDGE ON THE JONES FALLS EXPRESSWAY IN BALTIMORE WAS THE IMPETUS FOR A BOLD INITIATIVE BY THE MASSACHUSETTS TURNPIKE AUTHORITY TO REDESIGN THE COLORS FOR ALL THE BRIDGES ALONG THEIR MAJOR TOLL ROAD. (BRIDGE COLOR DESIGN BY STAN EDMISTER; PHOTOGRAPH BY ERIK KAVALSVICK.)

usual color treatment of bridges along the Jones Falls Expressway along Interstate 83 and wanted to learn more. A newspaper article about this project in *The New York Times* led her to public works artist Stan Edmister of Baltimore who was the source of this new concept. Edmister conceived the idea of designing a new color palette for repainting a series of bridges in Baltimore. Through extensive discussions, he convinced ten federal, state, and local agencies to agree to his novel idea.

Edmister's approach to bridge color design employs the newest technology in protective coatings, based on a high-gloss, polyurethane pigment-retentive paint system. He also accents certain bridge features using iridescent diffraction foil, most commonly used on reflective tape to make objects more visible at night. These foil strips are applied in selected locations to emphasize the structural elements of the bridge, such as vertical posts. Their subtle colors change as sunlight or car headlights are reflected on the foil.

Instead of the typical muted green or gray paint, these bridges offer citizens a subtle work of art in their public infrastructure. His work in Baltimore was supported by the National Endowment for the Arts and the Municipal Art Society. The designs were so successful they were featured in an exhibition in Baltimore City Hall. The invitations were issued jointly by the mayor of the city and the Municipal Art Society, an unusual collaboration between government and the art community and between bridge maintenance design and aesthetics.

Hershfang was determined to bring Edmister's artistic vision to Massachusetts. With the support of the Board of the Turnpike Authority, she invited Edmister to try his hand with the bridges and viaducts along the Turnpike. One of the first lessons Edmister imparted was that the Federal Highway Administration did not *require* all the bridges to be painted the same shade of green (known as Federal #595A-24172), but that it was simply accepted custom to use that color. In fact, the government had a surprising array of color samples which could be applied to bridges. This revelation makes one wonder how many other assumptions about public design could be changed. What is regulation and what is simply custom? Questioning each assumption often opens unexpected opportunities.

In contrast to many efforts in design advocacy, arguing about "excessive cost" of design and competing for scarce public dollars was not a major debate with this project. Bridge

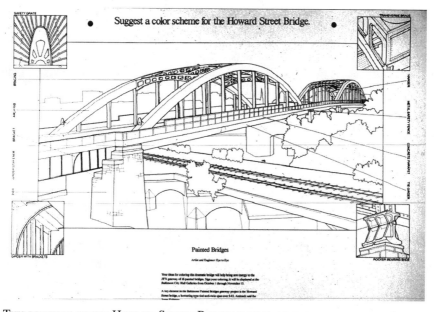

THIS DRAWING OF THE HOWARD STREET BRIDGE ENCOURAGED CITIZEN PARTICIPATION IN THE DESIGN PROCESS AS PEOPLE OFFERED THEIR OWN COLOR SCHEMES IN AN EXHIBITION SPONSORED BY THE MUNICIPAL ART SOCIETY AND THE MAYOR'S OFFICE IN BALTIMORE. (BRIDGE DRAWING BY STAN EDMISTER; PHOTOGRAPH BY ERIK KAVALSVICK.)

painting is a normal cost of maintenance for steel bridges, and the paint system proposed by Edmister actually saves the Turnpike Authority money. Although the cost of the paint per gallon is higher than the green or gray paint normally used, the newer paint system is superior in quality due to new technology and thus it lasts longer. Since labor is the largest portion of the cost of painting, the new paint system is actually more cost-efficient because the bridge painting will last several years longer.

Since Edmister's approach to design is collaborative with the surrounding community, he invited the author to work jointly on this effort as the project planner. One of our first tasks was to create an Advisory Committee for this project, comprised of personnel from the Turnpike engineering, landscaping, and maintenance departments, experts in public art and design, and community representatives. These members were considered by Edmister to be "partnership artists" to respond with him to opportunities, ideas, and his preliminary sketches and to ensure that the proposed design scheme appropriately reflected the surrounding community. From the inception of this project, community education and public outreach were considered critical to success.

The unusual combination of art and technology also made this project an ideal mechanism to introduce children to science, engineering, and aesthetics. As part of our application to the National Endowment for the Arts, which funded the design and planning stage of this project, we introduced a partnership with a nonprofit educational program known as the Massachusetts Pre-Engineering Program, or MassPEP. The primary mission of MassPEP is to motivate African-American, Hispanic, Native American, and female students in grades six through twelve to enter science, engineering, math-based, and technical careers. Hands-on learning is emphasized, along with student achievement through academic success, leadership ability, and improved self-confidence. Close coordination with teachers, the business community, and area universities helps make this program a success.

The technology and aesthetics of bridge design and color treatment were introduced to students in the MassPEP program through the public works artist and staff engineers of the Turnpike Authority. Working with middle-school students in the inner-city John D. O'Bryant School in Roxbury, a series of classroom and on-site activities brought the challenges of bridge design and engineering directly to the students, along with an appreciation of the diversity of possible professional careers previously unknown. With the assistance of Wentworth Institute, the students also had an opportunity to learn about bridge aesthetics through hands-on computer technology as they chose color designs for their own bridges.

A short video was produced describing the process and outcome of this bridge design project. The video is used as an important tool in educating the public about the potential for improved bridge design, as well as other state or local public works and transportation agencies who may be looking for ways to expand their impact on the design of their community through transportation and art.

This project is an ideal example of opportunities to combine art and transportation. The application of new color design treatments to public works such as bridges, tunnels, and viaducts provides a large canvas for the artist's creativity while improving the surrounding visual environment. Sites should be chosen carefully, however, since excessive color design treatment could be overwhelming. Some areas are best left as passive background.

Like all collaborations between art and design, the best approach is to consider art involvement during the early phase of the design process, not afterwards. Since fewer new bridges are constructed these days, however, that ideal is not often possible. Including aesthetic color enhancements as part of the normal bridge maintenance and repainting process is therefore a desirable alternative.

Other Opportunities for Art and Transportation

State and local public agencies increasingly are recognizing the potential for collaborations between artists and transportation or public works agencies. The California Department of Transportation (known as Caltrans) and the California Arts Council, for example, cosponsored a successful conference entitled *Giving Transportation a Sense of Community: Transportation, Art and Design.* Over 35 projects were highlighted illustrating innovative partnerships between public agencies and artists, ranging from the public art program for the city of Seattle to the bridge and highway design programs described earlier in Massachusetts.

One particularly noteworthy project currently under way is a collaboration with an artist, neighborhood schoolchildren, and the Los Angeles County Metropolitan Transportation Authority's "Art for Rail Transit" Program. The artist, Joe Sam, was selected by a committee composed of community representatives and art professionals for an art installation along the Metro Green Line. Working with local schoolchildren who live adjacent to the new station, Sam led an intensive workshop to help each child complete a full-scale model of themselves on foam core. In a community event, the full-scale models were then lifted to the top of the sixteen- to twenty-foot columns high above passengers' heads at the Metro station for a temporary indication of the proposed public art work. The children's sketches were also exhibited at the shopping center located adjacent to the subway station. Based in part on the children's ideas, Sam will fabricate individual polychrome metal figures

THE ART FOR RAIL TRANSIT PROGRAM IN LOS ANGELES FEATURES AN INNOVATIVE PUBLIC ART COMPONENT WORKING WITH ARTIST JOE SAM AND NEIGHBORHOOD SCHOOLCHILDREN, AS ILLUSTRATED IN THIS DESIGN FOR THE METRO GREEN LINE. (A PROJECT OF THE METROPOLITAN TRANSPORTATION AUTHORITY'S ART FOR RAIL TRANSIT PROGRAM.)

which will be attached to the columns as sculptures in the station and adjacent parking lot. The project was developed in conjunction with five area schools and included an educational component for the children.

Public art was also used as a partial antidote to citizen outrage over the demolition of a six-kilometer strip of landscaping and flowers in the middle of a major roadway to Amsterdam, Holland, to make way for a new public transit project. A local artist, Lottie Buit, saw an opportunity to transform the stark concrete transit stations into places for art. She had the difficult job of convincing two municipalities, the adjacent cities of Amsterdam and Amstelveen, as well as the public transport agency, that her idea had merit. After extensive meetings, the three organizations agreed to work together, with the assistance of the Amsterdam Municipal Art Council who sponsored the competition to select artists to work on each of seven transit stations. Like many public art projects, the architectural designs had already been completed when the opportunity for art began.

Amsterdam public artist Lottie Buit conceived the idea of transforming stark concrete tram stations into a canvas for art. This work grew out of a neighborhood uproar when extensive landscaping along the roadway was removed to make way for a new railway line. (Public art by Lottie Buit at a transit station in Amstelveen, Holland.)

According to Buit, the process would have been improved if their design work occurred concurrently. The roadway is now enhanced by artwork painted on the previously stark concrete buildings, providing a new visual identity and landmark for the transit stations. This project provided an additional opportunity for Buit to work on designs for public art now placed directly on the tram buses which travel throughout Amsterdam.

Why Work with Artists?

For transportation and public works officials, the prospect of working with artists on projects may seem daunting and overwhelming. You may think: What can artists offer experts in public works? How can artists responsibly propose designs without a thorough grounding in engineering and public safety? What if a controversial scheme is proposed which threatens the community's sense of aesthetics? Isn't it easier and safer to work solely with engineers who understand our technical requirements?

Public agencies benefit in unexpected ways from working with artists. Artists and designers are used to solving complex problems with limited resources in innovative ways. They often look at old problems in a new manner with a different point of view. Artists historically find new expressions by reflecting the community around them, and that trait can generate exciting new applications for transportation and public works.

Collaborations between artists and transportation or public works projects work best if there is open communication between the public agency, engineers, the planners, the artist, and representatives of the community. Public agency involvement must include more than the agency director. The relevant engineering staff and the maintenance crew must be equally involved. The maintenance staff particularly has critical insight into materials, implementation, and long-term care of the project. Working with the engineers and technical staff of the agency will help ensure that public safety and structural concerns are met. Often these collaborations can produce new approaches in design as the engineers and artists inform each other about the latest in technology or new application of existing materials and procedures.

The advantages to the artist in working on public transportation projects are numerous. Perhaps the most compelling is the opportunity to work on a much larger canvas with the larger landscapes and infrastructure of highways, bridges, and public transit. The impact of the artists' work is greater than that of more individual collections, museums, or galleries. Finally, the budgets for transportation projects are much larger than typical art or design efforts.

Artists and public works agencies do face unexpected frustrations in these collaborations, however. Initially both sides must learn to communicate with different language, different technologies, and a different creative process of conceptualizing and implementing their work. An individual painting may be completed in six weeks or six months, for example, where a bridge may not be designed and built for twelve years. Transportation and public works projects must conform to extensive federal, state, and local regulations and procedures. With public bidding requirements, the artist cannot control who will actually be constructing the final design. The need to compromise is essential, and many artists are not comfortable with that requirement. The public agency, in addition, must be open to new ideas and to new approaches to solving old problems.

Many public agencies may be receptive to partnerships with artists, but they do not know where to begin. The best approach is to select a partner who brings knowledge in public art and a willingness to collaborate. Often a state or local arts agency is a good place to start. Ad hoc advisory groups composed of experts in public art, transportation, community planning, and design are useful. Select a prominent site and clearly define the scope and expectations of the project. Be careful how the artist and designer (or team) are selected, be reasonable about the budget, and make sure technical considerations are well understood. Involve the public agency from the top leadership through to the engineering, maintenance, and public information staff. Be open to new ideas, anticipate problems, but don't be afraid of change. With good communication and creative thinking on all sides, the results will be surprisingly rewarding.

Lessons Learned

With any public project, the process is often lengthy and can succumb to changes in leadership. The political process is dynamic. A change in government can result in new priorities and working styles. The game plan for a project can change unexpectedly, which is frustrating for all parties. In some cases this change is extremely productive, however, if new leadership recognizes the validity of design collaborations or initiatives which previously floundered.

Involving community representatives will help ensure that the project reflects the character of the neighborhood and will be more readily accepted upon completion. This involvement should be more than viewing finished drawings in order to secure neighborhood approval. Citizen representatives should have an opportunity to respond to earlier schematic drawings and to express their concerns or questions. Not every project will be of a scale to require citizen involvement, but the more public or visible a project, the more benefits from community involvement. Public art and transportation projects also benefit from public forums which present the proposed collaboration. Targeted sessions with schoolchildren to educate them about the project can also be valuable. Working with children has the multiple advantages of exposing them to challenging ideas, having them challenge *your* ideas, getting their input on proposed projects, introducing them to new career opportunities, and possibly informing their parents about a new project.

The key is to find the spark of creativity in the director or board of an agency and then capitalize on that energy, preferably by pursuing plans which meet the priorities of the leadership as well as your own.

Chapter 4

Using Money as an Incentive: Supporting Design through Grant Programs

Education, recognition, and technical assistance are essential in supporting quality design, but at times nothing succeeds like cold, hard cash. Money, such as grants and awards, provides incentives for education or development of new approaches to old problems. The Massachusetts Council on the Arts and Humanities' Design and Development Program created two major funding initiatives specifically for the design of cities and towns. The Community Design Assistance Program targeted cities participating in the state's Main Street Program, and the Rural Design Assistance Program was created especially for small towns. This chapter describes the process of creating these programs and highlights other important national models to offer interesting lessons and models for others to adapt.

Recipients of grant funds emphasize that the benefits go far beyond the dollars received. These communities are empowered by state recognition of their locally initiated projects. The technical assistance and the funding serve as catalysts for action. Even cities unable to receive state funding found that the *process* of applying for Council grants forced the community to:

- Articulate its concerns
- Define the town's goals

- Obtain consensus on town priorities and needs
- Agree on a plan of action
- Identify the talent and resources necessary to implement the plan

Although the steps listed above are valuable for any planning process, do not be misled. Towns spent extensive time and energy trying to secure Council funds, and they were not pleased when the Board of Directors did not approve their grant proposal. The process of applying for state funds did offer an opportunity to evaluate difficult and important issues, provided communities with valuable technical assistance in addressing their concerns, and generated a forum to identify solutions vital to the future well-being of the town.

Getting Started

Our first foray into design funding was a small-scale program funded through a grant from the National Endowment for the Arts to the Massachusetts Council on the Arts and Humanities. The Council had no experience giving grants for design directly to cities and towns, and we decided to test the waters through a pilot program. We tested our concept and solicited project ideas within the state by contacting colleagues in other state agencies familiar with communities' planning needs. None of the other state agencies had a funding program in design, but they were all aware of communities desperately in need of assistance. The gap in public support was painfully obvious, and we worked hard to fill that need. As we stated in our funding application to the National Endowment for the Arts:

The Council is aware that the earliest stage of a development project is often the most difficult. A sound idea may be identified to meet the community's needs, but how can you test the feasibility of the plan? How can you convince the City Council, the local bank, or the public financing agency that the funds should be allocated for this new proposal? Money is often unavailable at this critical stage. It is here that architectural design studies should be undertaken and urban design guidelines enacted, for all too frequently the effects of poor planning are evident only after construction is under way.

We asked twelve communities to submit a short proposal describing how they would use Council design funds. We then picked the two most intriguing projects and applied to the National Endowment for the Arts for funding on their behalf. The town of Pepperell, a small community in northern Massachusetts, identified several architectural and historically significant buildings that they wanted to convert into municipal office space and housing for the elderly. The city of Beverly, a seacoast community north of Boston, had a decaying downtown center with potential for revitalization. The city wanted to develop urban design guidelines for the area surrounding a large former industrial mill in anticipation of redevelopment.

This small-scale funding effort gave the Council an inkling of town government procedures and concern about design of their public environment. Council funds definitely served as a catalyst for action, although each project required significant staff time for oversight and administration. In addition, the need to drastically revise the Council budgetary forms and requirements (developed for arts and humanities organizations) became all too clear as we tried to adapt them to municipal requirements and procedures. The Design and Development Program later streamlined the Council's application and budgetary forms dramatically to simplify them and provide clear directions. This major achievement was quickly negated the next year, however, when the application forms and budget requirements for all the funding programs of the Council were computerized, and we were required to adapt our materials to that format.

The response to the modest trial balloon of the pilot project reflected a serious demand for a community design funding program. The Council did not have extensive resources to allocate to a new program. Although the staff and Board were consistently supportive of our efforts, the Design and Development Program faced the budgetary battles of being "the new kid on the block," particularly within an agency that saw the arts, not design, as its main mandate. Since we had limited resources, a small staff, and a state with extensive need for assistance, we had to be strategic in targeting our resources. We did not want to raise false expectations around the state of "we're from the government and we're here to help you" when we knew the pot of money was relatively small. We were also juggling two other major state pilot projects and long-range planning to get the new Design and Development Program off the ground. We simply had to find an efficient and effective mechanism to implement this new funding program.

Early research pointed to a strong need for a funding program to meet the needs of older urban communities in Massachusetts. We wanted to ensure geographic diversity across the state, target lower to moderate-income populations, and ideally work in areas where local staff and officials could ably carry out the results of projects funded by the Council. We saw no merit in funding a program that would only result in reports that sat on shelves. We also wanted to be sure we did not duplicate other programs available elsewhere.

A Partnership with Main Streets

After carefully surveying existing resources and programs available in the region, we proposed a partnership with the Main Streets Program of the Commonwealth's Executive Office of Communities and Development. The Main Street Program, originally created by the National Trust for Historic Preservation, worked toward economic revitalization of the central business districts of older downtowns. The Main Street Program emphasized storefront improvements, competitive marketing, good management, and historic preservation of significant buildings. Through the Council's new "Community Design Assistance Program," we piggybacked on the Main Street Program to add a strong overlay of design awareness. To our knowledge, it was the first time two state agencies collaborated on a funding program of this nature.

Eligible applicants to the Council's first full funding program in design were communities participating in the state's Main Street Program. This partnership provided several advantages for us. First, the eligible applicants met our stated criteria of income, geographic diversity, and need. In addition, most of the communities demonstrated a desire to work on downtown improvement and identified important historic buildings for revitalization. The existence of the ongoing Main Street Program also saved us enormous effort in targeting and educating potential applicants to our new program since they were well defined and contained in size.

Our biggest challenge was educating the Main Street coordinators about the possibilities for design improvement in their communities. They were well versed in issues related to economic or commercial development, but for many, city design was outside their expertise. We held workshops around the state and spent much time listening to their concerns, helping them to understand existing opportunities for change, and just talking about the language of design and cities. The videotape *Places as Art* was a useful tool for this purpose.[9] Some of the Main Street managers showed the videotape to their constituents and partners, thus expanding our educational and advocacy efforts.

Tangible Results from Communities

The Main Street communities applied for assistance on projects related to downtown revitalization. A design panel of experts reviewed all the proposals and made recommendations to the Council Board of Directors for approval. The scope of projects funded ranged from the city of Holyoke's creation of a design review process to the city of Lynn's plan for landscape improvements linking residential urban neighborhoods and their Main Street area.

As an example of one project's results, Holyoke produced a *Downtown Design Guidebook* with the assistance of Centerbrook Architect and Planners that offered design information relating to historic buildings, including building-by-building recommendations for improvement and information on the town's facade grant program. The technical companion to this

THE *DOWNTOWN DESIGN GUIDEBOOK* DEVELOPED ESSENTIAL GUIDANCE FOR THE CITY OF HOLYOKE IN IMPROVING ITS CITY CENTER. THE NATIONAL MAIN STREET PROGRAM PROVIDED IMPORTANT MODELS. (REPRINTED WITH PERMISSION FROM *THE BUILDING IMPROVEMENT FILE*. COPYRIGHT © 1978, NATIONAL TRUST FOR HISTORIC PRESERVATION, NATIONAL MAIN STREET CENTER.)

guidebook benefited from information from the National Main Street Center. The city distributed the manual to property owners, aldermen, the building codes department, the planning board, and other municipal offices. Considered a first step as an educational tool toward implementing a more formalized design review process, the manual became a model for other communities.

Pittsfield used its grant to create a facade design program for downtown buildings and to prepare design guidelines for building renovation. The guidelines for "the care and feeding of old buildings" were distributed widely, and like Holyoke's manual, were requested frequently by other communities.

Over and over again, we heard pleas for more information from other communities. Although these towns are not the first to create design guidelines or prepare useful manuals, in the past the resources almost never were shared properly from town to town (and certainly not from state to state). In addition to educating community groups and businesses, the process of creating a manual served an important educational role for the public officials and staff involved.

One of the most influential projects funded by the Community Design Assistance Program was the master plan for urban design of street and sidewalk improvements for the Roslindale neighborhood in Boston. This relatively small grant to Roslindale's Main Street Program allowed them to influence the design of over a million dollars worth of public improvements that the city of Boston implemented in Roslindale Village. The Roslindale Main Street Program set up a designer selection team that included citizens in the process, in addition to representatives from the Public Facilities Department, the Massachusetts Bay Transit Authority, and the Public Works Department. According to the Main Street Director, Kathleen McCabe, including citizens, city officials, architects, and engineers in a designer selection team was an innovative idea to the city of Boston. The city was so impressed with the community group's involvement that they requested their assistance in later projects.

Providing Aid to Small Towns

An important outgrowth of the Community Design Assistance Program was recognition of the emerging needs of small towns

THE RURAL DESIGN ASSISTANCE PROGRAM HELPED COMMUNITIES ACROSS THE STATE GRAPPLE WITH COMPLEX ISSUES RELATED TO PRESERVATION, GROWTH, AND COMMUNITY IDENTITY. (COURTESY OF THE CENTER FOR RURAL MASSACHUSETTS; DESIGN BY KEVIN WILSON AND HARRY DODSON.)

in the state. The design panel reviewing grant applications urged the Council to expand the program to help the numerous small towns in the state facing extreme development pressures too complex to handle alone.

The Rural Design Assistance Program was created to help small towns make their own informed decisions by providing funds for projects in the areas of architecture, landscape architecture, and planning. The Council wanted to help small towns help themselves by identifying their own goals and then guiding development and/or preserving the special character of their communities. Examples of difficult questions small towns ask include:

- Should we encourage or prevent new development?
- How do we tackle the essential need for farmland preservation in the context of development demand?
- How can we best handle traffic and environmental pressures?
- How do we reconcile conflicting views of the future character and identity of our town by long-time and recent residents?

Several categories of projects could be funded through the Rural Design Assistance Program, relating to design process, strategies, feasibility studies, and site design. These categories were summarized in the program guidelines as follows:

• *Design process* to aid community understanding of the existing character of the town and to define future goals for its shape. For example, community workshops could be held to identify key design issues for a specific parcel of land or for the town as a whole.

• *Design strategies* to guide the shape, quality, and character of physical change, incorporating the cultural, historic, and physical character of the town and surrounding rural landscape. For example, a town might develop design guidelines, design review procedures, or rural landscape management techniques to be used as part of the municipal planning process.

• *Design feasibility* studies for preservation or creative use or reuse of significant buildings or areas. Feasibility studies, for example, can explore how a group of buildings or public open spaces can best be reused or redesigned.

• *Site design* to guide development in a critical geographic area or parcel of land, such as an area faced with increasing development pressures or an area which is particularly critical to maintaining the appropriate aesthetic and/or physical character of the town.

The Rural Design Assistance Program was the only program the Council targeted to small towns and one of only a few in the state with a population restriction. Cities or towns with a population of 10,000 or less were eligible to apply. The population eligibility was later raised to 15,000 to include additional towns facing development pressures. Two or more towns could apply jointly for a project of mutual concern, and the funding limits for joint proposals were increased. At the time, approximately 60% of the cities and towns had populations of 10,000 or less, and of that total over half had populations of 5,000 or less. Many of these towns, furthermore, felt ignored by the state and lost in the shadows of the bigger cities.

The need for state assistance was clear. What wasn't as obvious was the way to help communities articulate their concerns and then develop a plan to solve them. Most of the smaller towns had no professional planning or design staff. The development pressures and related controversies were hard enough; devising solutions seemed almost impossible. Council staff had numerous conversations with potential applicants in which we talked for an hour just trying to help them put words to the complex problems the town faced.

Extensive conversations, technical assistance, and workshops around the state were essential to target the communities' needs. Identifying these goals and then obtaining community consensus on the best way to reach them were often the greatest obstacles the towns faced. The Council contracted with the Center for Rural Massachusetts from the University of Massachusetts in Amherst to provide critical technical assistance and guidance. The Associate Director of the Center, Randall Arendt, provided invaluable service helping towns identify their concerns and some possible solutions.

Workshops and public information

Similar to the approach used for the Community Design Assistance Program, the Design and Development Department organized workshops around the state to tell towns about this new program and to educate them about rural design. The Center for Rural Massachusetts gave an excellent slide presentation on design of towns. After seeing this lecture once, observers said they could never look at their neighborhood in the same way again. We outlined the goals and requirements of the Rural Design Assistance Program, explained what we could and could not fund in as clear and nonbureaucratic terms as possible, and gave tips on grantsmanship. An important part of these workshops for many of the participants was the presentation on how to select the best designers for their projects.

Workshops were held in various locations throughout the state, but always at sites that were well located, well designed, accessible for people with physical disabilities, and known to the general community. Press announcements were made in anticipation of each meeting, and wide public notice was secured. The Rural Design Assistance Program generated more response from the press than any other program in the Council's history. Each step of the grant application process was documented in town newspapers, from the Council holding workshops, to the town's application, preliminary approval, and results of the final Council decision. I often thought that even if the Council could not fund *any* projects, the extensive press coverage accomplished a great deal in raising public awareness about rural design.

A two-stage application process

We were well aware of the lack of staff resources in the small towns and tried to make the application process as painless as possible. (Unfortunately, our own state bureaucracy hindered some of our best efforts in this regard.) In order to simplify the application process, we asked towns to submit a two-page preliminary application so we could determine if their application was eligible or competitive before they went to the effort required for our standard application.

This two-stage process was extremely helpful in advising communities when they were requesting funds for ineligible projects or for proposals which we knew would never get approvals by our panel of experts or the Board. For example, many towns needed funds to redesign the interior office space of their town hall; but that use did not meet the goals of the Program, nor was it a particularly competitive proposal idea. We had no interest in wasting their time or ours; we were eager for results which helped the towns. This two-stage process allowed us to provide additional technical assistance to communities as they refined their proposal for the final application.

In the second stage, a more extensive description of the proposed project, the qualifications of the selected design team, and the estimated budget were required. The Council selected a design panel with expertise in architecture, landscape design, planning, and historic preservation to review all the applications. The panel made funding recommendations to the Board of Directors of the Council, which was responsible for the final funding decisions.

The funding criteria for selection of recipients as described in the Council guidelines is presented below:

- Improvement of the rural environment; potential to aid in guiding appropriate development and/or preserving the special character of the community and surrounding rural landscape
- Quality of the selected designer or design team, including expertise and ability to accomplish the design proposal
- Potential to involve and mobilize the community in the cre-

ation and implementation of the project; well-advertised
public planning and selectmen's meetings must be held prior
to submission of the proposal in order to encourage community input and awareness of the project
- Evidence of commitment by the town to implement and
  maintain the results of the design project
- Realistic and detailed timeline, work plan, and budget
- Four letters of support from community members or organizations directly involved or affected by the project

Selecting the Best Designers

Since one of the goals of the Design and Development Program
was to improve the quality of design of the public environment
in the Commonwealth, we emphasized that all projects must be
completed by qualified and talented designers. A town could
propose the most innovative project imaginable, but if an infe-
rior designer received the commission, the results could be disastrous. We were not looking for the "name" designers, but we
did look for talent.

Much to the chagrin of the cities and towns, we required
them to identify the designers with whom they would work as
part of the application process to the Council. We received the
most complaints about this requirement, and understandably
so. Applicants were always understaffed, and as they repeatedly said to us, "If we don't get the Council funds, we will have
wasted all that time trying to pick an architect."

Our response was always the same. We emphasized that
the quality of the outcome of their project depends in large part
on the quality of the proposed design team, and the panel requires that information in order to judge the project.

Since the towns knew they would be judged on the quality
of the proposed designers, they worked hard to find the best
talent possible. Often this relationship continued after the
tenure of the Rural Design Project. Although many communities would have preferred that we did not have this requirement, they often told us that they learned important information from the architects as they went through the designer
selection procedure. The most useful tips on selecting quality
designers presented in our regional workshops to communities
are summarized in the accompanying window in the hope they
will be useful to others.

TIPS IN THE SELECTION OF DESIGNERS

1. After defining the proposed project, determine the type of designer or design team needed for the anticipated outcome.

2. Carefully assess the scope of work to be completed. Be clear about defining goals and anticipated results for the project.

3. Devise an accurate and realistic work plan and budget.

4. Ensure that all local regulations for selection of consultants are met.

5. Inform all relevant local community departments and organizations prior to advertising your project.

6. Determine how decision making will occur and who has ultimate responsibility and control.

7. Depending on the scale of your project, advertise your request for proposals in local and regional newspapers and professional journals. Ask colleagues and other communities for names of talented designers, and send them a request for a proposal.

8. Prepare a more detailed description of the project to send to potential designers after they express initial interest. Include a summary of the sponsoring organization, a description of the proposed project, information about the site and the community, your estimated time frame and budget, and a description of the scope of services. Outline the general work plan expected of the designer and any final products. Proposals can be judged more evenly if requested information is presented in a fairly consistent format.

9. Responses to proposals should clearly describe the design team, their individual qualifications, and exactly who will be working on the project and for what amount of time (including any subcontractors). Be wary of proposals which suggest that the "star" or "name" designer will do all the work, unless you can verify this fact. (Often it is not necessary or advisable to pay for the most experienced person's time for all of the work anyway.) Designers should submit descriptions or evidence of prior work relevant to your project, but they should not be asked to submit a preliminary design as part of their submission materials.

10. References are essential. Request names and phone numbers of at least three references, and then call them. Ask for a frank and confidential response from the references. Be sure to ask if they would hire the designer again and see how enthusiastically they answer. Ask

about the designer's professionalism, ability to work within a given budget and time schedule, responsiveness to concerns and problems, and ability to communicate and work with others. If possible, make a site visit and look at examples of completed work.

11. Personal interviews are vital. A chemistry that works or one that explodes will mean success or failure for the project. Select the top three to five proposals and schedule interviews. Request that the actual individuals who will work on your project be present. Don't let fancy slide shows dominate the proceedings, but rather use the time to ask questions which will let you get a handle on the personalities and qualities of the people who will be giving you advice for the future of your community.

12. Asking the right questions is always important. Some suggested questions to ask are listed below, but interviewers will have their own priorities and concerns. The following questions are meant as guides to help elicit information useful for picking the best designer for your project:

- Describe a project or two that you completed which will provide the most experience for our town's proposal. What lessons did you learn that would have relevance for us? What problems did you encounter, and how did you solve them?

- From your experience, can you give us advice on where our proposed scope of work, time line, or budget needs improvement or revision? Can you work within the framework we outlined?

- You indicated how you would approach the problem outlined in our Request for Proposals. (Now ask a specific question related to their approach.)

- How would our project fit within the work plan of your office? How much of your time would be spent managing this project, and who else would be working on it? What are their qualifications?

- Have you or your firm experienced any legal or professional difficulties? How were they resolved?

- What do you foresee as the most difficult aspect of our project? How do you expect to handle it?

- What part of this project do you expect to be the most rewarding to you? Why?

If a project is particularly complex or unusual, or if a large number of responses is anticipated, you may choose to hold a meeting soon after issuing the Request for Proposals. Include the meeting notice in the advertising. This meeting will give you an opportunity to answer questions at one session, saving you countless phone calls and giving all the potential consultants the benefit of hearing the answers to the questions of others. The meeting could also be a chance for you to hear if you have drastically underestimated the budget or overestimated the scope of work, or if perhaps your understanding of the type of work required is not accurate. You may have to redefine and readvertise your project, but it is much better to make that decision *before* you receive the proposals.

Typical Mistakes in Defining the Problem

A problem can't be solved unless it is correctly identified. The most frequent mistake towns made in defining their project for the Rural Design Assistance Program was asking designers to solve a problem which was outlined much too broadly. Often that problem occurred when the town tried to solve too many problems at once. People couldn't agree on the most pressing issue, so they would compromise by combining all the questions into one proposal for some unsuspecting designer to solve. That type of compromise is almost always a mistake; usually everyone is unhappy with the outcome. Another related error is that of asking an architect to solve a problem which is really more of a landscape or traffic engineering dilemma. These skills are not interchangeable.

Judging the scale and cost of a project is possibly one of the most difficult questions for communities in the process of hiring consultants. Towns may present a problem to their consultant that could take a year and $150,000 in fees to accomplish, yet they need it in three months and have only $25,000 to allocate. By being extremely clear about the nature of the required product and talking to other towns and consultants who have completed similar efforts elsewhere, you may be able to better gauge your own project. Projects that are clearly focused with questions well framed are more likely to produce successful results.

SOLVE THE RIGHT PROBLEM.

Another mistake that communities typically make is misjudging citizens' opinions of the most pressing design problem. Town officials may determine that design plans for a new industrial or commercial complex are needed, for example, but the residents may have vastly different ideas about the future of their hometown. Often, citizens do not articulate this vision until *after* the town or developers spend thousands of dollars and many months on plans and studies. Controversies become crystallized when people fear a specific development or see the bulldozers breaking ground. It is much wiser to work with the community to agree on a plan for future growth, development, and preservation *prior* to the arrival of the bulldozers. Public officials, planners, and citizens can engage in a much more rational discussion at that point.

DEFINE YOUR COMMUNITY'S VISION OF THE FUTURE *BEFORE* THE BULLDOZERS ARRIVE.

More than one proposal to the Rural Design Assistance Program ended in failure because town officials thought they knew what the public wanted, and spent countless hours of their time (and ours) on the project, only to have it end in controversy or inaction because it did not meet the broader scope of the residents' view of their town. This dilemma occurred even though we required documentation of support for the proposal. The unfortunate lesson learned is that the loudest voices of dissent often occur *after* a project is under way. Controversy is often difficult to avoid completely. Early citizen participation and education are worth the extra time and effort.

Expanded Advocacy through Design Education

The educational impact of the Rural Design Assistance Program became increasingly apparent. This program offered unparalleled opportunities for children to learn about their communities, their history, and their future. Students could witness or participate in the planning and implementation of design projects which affect their hometowns. Schoolchildren also had the potential to educate their families through school projects.

As an incentive to towns, we offered increased funding to pay for a design education component which had direct relevance to their overall project. Council funds could be used for curriculum planning, a design education consultant or professional, and related classroom or transportation expenses. We held separate workshops that described design education possibilities around the state to educate towns about opportunities related to their projects. In addition, the Council's *Guidebook to Selected Projects in Design Education* provided examples and advice.

One prime example of design education projects funded by the Rural Design Assistance Program related to the town of Hull's efforts to create urban design guidelines for an intensively used beachfront area known as Nantasket. Educators used an interdisciplinary approach to introduce seventh- and eighth-graders to basic concepts underlying the design and development process. Students observed Planning Board and Design Review Board hearings and then participated in role-playing activities, taking on the parts of various players in the development scenario.

The town of Wendell's rural design project evaluated the design impact of flexible zoning bylaws. Citizens were involved through extensive community meetings and a tour of the town during which they photographed sites of importance or concern and sketched and labeled maps to show their findings. Students also participated in the process by designing a new playground. They learned firsthand of the compromises necessary to articulate their dreams of the playground and then consider what it takes to make them a reality, grappling with spatial, environmental, and financial concerns.

Results of Funded Projects

The Rural Design Assistance Program was successful in generating a wide variety of projects across the Commonwealth. The list in the accompanying window reflects the range and diversity of funded projects. These Massachusetts towns may be contacted directly to learn more about these projects. Some of these projects are also described briefly below.

Projects Funded by the Rural Design Assistance Program

Belchertown	Landscape management measures to help the New England Small Farm Institute protect the Lampson Brook Valley
Buckland	Alternative development approaches for the Clemson Brook Valley
Charlemont and Shelburne	Site plan review and design standards for the Mohawk Trail
Colrain	Townscape plan for Colrain City, the village center
Edgartown	Design standards for the downtown business district
Granby	Design guidelines and requirements for commercial and residential development along Route 202
Hadley	Feasibility study for restoration of the historic North Hadley Village Hall
Hanson	Master plan for reuse of the town-owned Camp Kiwanee
Hull	Urban design guidelines for development of Nantasket
Lancaster	Evaluation of the historic town library as part of guidelines for the town's municipal complex
Leyden	Community character attitude survey of town qualities valued by residents which informed design criteria developed for each land type; development of a zoning overlay district to protect the town's scenic and community resources
New Salem	Reuse plan for the 30-acre New Salem Academy site as part of the reconstructed historic town common
Nantucket and Williamstown	Design concepts for rural subdivision regulations
Northborough	Restoration study for an aqueduct and bridge
Northfield	Identification of community goals for design and land use management for Main Street
Orleans	Design and regulatory strategies for Town Cove
Plympton	Community education was followed by a land use management strategy and design guidelines
Provincetown	Computer graphic simulation of design and development alternatives for the town
Stockbridge	Restoration of the historic Butler Bridge
Townsend	Reuse plan for the town hall
Wendell	Evaluation of the design impact of flexible zoning bylaws
Wenham	Creation of a conference, videotape, and publication to increase awareness of the town's needs and future direction
West Newbury	Design of a nature park for the elderly
Williamsburg	Creation of bylaws preserving distinctive architectural and landscape qualities of the town

The New England Small Farm Institute and the town of Belchertown explored innovative land management procedures in order to protect the important Lampson Brook Valley. Nantucket, an island town off the southeastern Massachusetts coast, and Williamstown, a town on the opposite end of the state, worked together to develop design concepts for rural subdivision regulations for their respective communities. The town of Plympton focused on community education that resulted in a land use management strategy and design guidelines. West Newbury used their Rural Design Assistance grant to design a nature park to benefit the elderly who lived nearby. Provincetown explored the impact of future growth through computer graphic simulation of alternative design and development strategies for their town. The town of Wenham created a townwide forum, a video, and a community handbook to serve as a major planning document for the next five years. The handbook was delivered to every resident's door by the local Boy Scouts.

Each community had unique needs and a different approach to design education, advocacy, and technical assistance. In sum, town-wide conferences, concerns, and issues were hotly debated, buildings and landscapes were saved and rejuvenated for future generations, and guidelines, bylaws, and design manuals were prepared, implemented, and shared with other communities.

EVERY LITTLE BIT HELPS: TO HELP PAY FOR RENOVATION OF TOWNSEND'S PUBLIC LIBRARY, THE LOCAL HARDWARE STORE HAD A PAINT SALE. FOR EACH GALLON OF PAINT PURCHASED, THE STORE DONATED ANOTHER GALLON TO REPAINT THE LIBRARY. OTHER SIMILAR DONATIONS INCREASED THE SCOPE OF THE PROJECT AND THE FEELING OF INVESTMENT AND PRIDE BY CITIZENS IN THE COMMUNITY.

One of the aspects of this program that was most rewarding to the Council was the degree to which the smaller towns showed their appreciation. They were often amazed when state officials would come all the way out to their town for public meetings and workshops. (The typical expectation was that all events occurred in Boston.) When we made site visits to present the funding awards the town hall would be filled with people. Volunteers who worked so hard on proposals would take time off from work, bake homemade cookies for a reception with the state officials, and share powerful stories about the impact of the particular project on their community. Their response was extremely touching.

Other Innovative Partnerships with Main Streets

The impact of partnerships with Main Street Programs and small towns can be far-reaching. Other successful models demonstrate the results of collaborations between state arts agencies and Main Street Programs. These models could be adapted on a local or regional level as well. The most important factor is identification of dedicated leaders within the two organizations who want to work together to establish the new initiative and who share compatible goals for the program.

DesignWorks Program

The impetus for a statewide initiative in design targeting small towns was first identified in a major conference entitled *Design Oklahoma* sponsored by the State Arts Council of Oklahoma. The Council brought together leaders in design, the arts, and community planning to meet each other and to explore the possibility of creating a new statewide design program. The participants tallied the resources most urgently needed in the state: leadership, good examples, technical assistance, and information about design.

In response, the State Arts Council of Oklahoma joined hands with the Oklahoma Main Street Program of the Oklahoma Department of Commerce to develop the DesignWorks program. This project was the first opportunity for these disparate state agencies to work together. The first task for each agency was to understand the language, the jargon, and the mission of the other. The Department of Commerce's incentive in this partnership was to improve the business climate of the state, since the objective of its Main Street Program was to improve the downtown viability of communities while improving their historic integrity. The State Arts Council wanted to create a new program to encourage the best in community design. These agencies tapped their expertise, their best staff, and their commitment to their respective concerns to create an important new program for the state.

Instead of grants, DesignWorks provides technical advice and assistance. Implementation of any projects identified must occur through the resources of the community requesting advice. Upon request from the community, the DesignWorks program will send a team of design professionals to meet with representatives of the town. The resource team is comprised of an architect, a landscape architect, a staff person from the Main Street Program, and the DesignWorks coordinator. The team works closely with the communities in a two-day intensive workshop, touring the town, meeting with a wide cross section of residents, and recommending a specific project as a practical example of how design can be integrated into strategic community planning.

To further their goal of public education and advocacy, the DesignWorks program staff initiated a video on public design. The Oklahoma State University Cooperative Extension Service became another valuable partner by producing the video *DesignWorks,* which is distributed to communities as a valuable tool in attracting support for public design projects. The video is distributed free of charge through the statewide County Extension offices and through the DesignWorks program. A resource book entitled *Community Design Book* also provides essential information related to architecture, landscape architecture, urban planning, and graphic design in an extremely accessible manner for use by citizens who want to improve their neighborhoods or downtown centers.

The DesignWorks program gives communities technical assistance, leaving them with a specific plan of action and resource tools to help in implementation. The program also provides the State Arts Council with unprecedented access to rural communities and gives them insight into design and the arts. DesignWorks has forged unexpected partnerships between state and local agencies responsible for business, economic development, historic preservation, the arts, and agriculture throughout Oklahoma.

Pride in Place

One of the most ambitious collaborations in design advocacy and education occurred through a three-state partnership: the

A DRAWING FROM *COMMUNITY DESIGN BOOK*, A PUBLICATION OFFERED BY THE OKLA-HOMA DESIGNWORKS PROGRAM. (COURTESY OF THE OKLAHOMA STATE ARTS COUNCIL.)

state arts councils and Main Street Programs of North Carolina, South Carolina, and Tennessee. Funded in part by the National Endowment for the Arts, the Pride in Place program provided extensive technical assistance to small towns in this region. The program was created to help small towns in which there is a particular need for public officials and citizens to understand how planning, zoning, and other design decisions influence the future of their community.

Resource teams visited these small towns after specific requests were made to address defined issues generally related to design, community planning, or cultural development. The resource teams helped the communities identify a plan of action to address their concerns and left the town a written strategy for action to be implemented by the locality.

The evaluation of Pride in Place offers several important lessons, drawn from their success, which would be replicable for others:

- Clearly define the expectations of the program and the community.
- Establish the correct fit between the skills and background of the resource team and the main concerns of the community.
- Conduct a preliminary site visit for a better understanding of key issues, types of experts to invite, and preparation of the resource team.
- Closely involve community residents and leaders in the process.
- Leave the community with a clear summary of the findings of the resource team with suggestions on implementation.
- Provide mechanisms for implementing the resource teams' recommendations, if possible, such as follow-up visits by the resource team and/or incentive grants.

Although Pride in Place no longer exists as a regional program, the North Carolina and South Carolina Arts Councils have created separate grant programs which provide design assistance to communities. The South Carolina Arts Commission established Community Designs, which is a partnership between the Commission and the South Carolina Downtown Development Association. The North Carolina Arts Council provides design assistance through its Management and Technical Assistance Program.

Two examples illustrate the impact of this program. The residents of Elizabethton in the mountains of Tennessee were concerned about the future of their small town in the face of environmental and development pressures. The Main Street Program of Elizabethton and the town's Community Development Department requested assistance from Pride in Place. After extensive interviews with community residents, planning, and evaluation, the resource team made several recommendations which were later implemented. These improvements included creation of a riverfront park to control erosion and provide public access to the river, planning an industrial park at one end of the main street to strengthen the economic base of the community, establishing a downtown design district, improving certain pedestrian amenities and building facades, and expanding the historic district.

A new community organization, the Rocky Mount/Edgecombe Community Development Corporation, was created to revitalize a row of condemned buildings in a historic district of Rocky Mount, North Carolina. The North Carolina Arts Council Design Assistance Program enabled the community group to include the arts in the critical early stages of the planning process. Public art became an essential unifying force for the project as well as for the town, which traditionally was divided between black and white racial neighborhoods. The new mixed-use development in the center of town will include a lively mix of shops, restaurants, offices, housing for the elderly, and public spaces. Artwork will highlight the history and culture of the residents of Rocky Mount.

As evident in these examples, programs providing an incentive for community action can make a big difference. Many communities need technical assistance mainly to help identify the right problem to tackle, followed by sage advice on how to carry out the recommended solutions. In other cases, grant funding can serve as the catalyst for a community to address a difficult problem. In every case, working with citizens, public officials, and people knowledgeable about the issue at hand is essential. No one can do it alone.

Chapter 5

CREATING SPACE FOR ARTISTS AND CULTURAL ACTIVITY

Artists as Urban Pioneers

Artists have historically served as "urban pioneers," seeking undiscovered, affordable sites within cities suitable for their studios, which serve by default as their homes as well. Often these locations are not zoned for residential use but function exceptionally well as studios and work space. Artists move into an area, rehabilitate the buildings on limited budgets, and then bring life and activity into formerly unknown or abandoned parts of the city.

Within a few years, others recognize the value of these emerging neighborhoods. They follow artists into the area, buy and renovate the buildings, and the market price of the units in this now trendy neighborhood soon exceeds the ability of the artists to pay. The artists are forced to move elsewhere, once again beginning the arduous process of securing affordable living and working space. Although this process of neighborhood revitalization known as *gentrification* is healthy for the city economically, it is disastrous in human and financial dimensions for the individuals who took the initial risk. They must relocate due to the increased value of the neighborhood which they helped to create. The city also suffers culturally and financially as artists choose to move to other towns to live and work.

The Quandaries of Development

Artists, cultural organizations, and others seeking affordable real estate face a painful dilemma: high costs of living in the larger cities where many artists work make reasonable space difficult to locate. To the extent that affordable rental space can be found, changing market conditions and a trend toward renovation and resale for condominiums or higher priced housing force relocation of tenants. Often artists seeking mortgage loans are denied financing due to their sporadic sources of income or to banks' concern about the reliability of their future income levels.

Frequent relocation is difficult professionally and personally. The impact of frequent relocation has broader implications for institutions, such as theaters, galleries, and performance spaces, because audiences rely on physical and geographic familiarity with their favorite cultural organizations. Whether for an individual artist or a cultural organization, the cost of moving is high in terms of finances, identity, audience development, time, and psychological well-being.

For these reasons, many artists and cultural organizations take the ambitious step of constructing or renovating a building to suit their own individual needs. Like most people, they desire stability, identity, familiarity, and some degree of control over the costs and physical layout of their space. They want the freedom to adapt their surroundings to their unique needs. Not all of these goals are actually accomplished through ownership of a building, but most people enter the development process with that perception in mind.

Securing, developing, and maintaining space for working, creating, performing, and exhibiting is a difficult struggle for most artists and cultural organizations. Their expertise is in their particular discipline, not in the seemingly insurmountable world of finance, governmental regulations, and development. When directors of cultural facilities identify a need to add or renovate space, they must quickly become experts in these complex arenas. The road to that knowledge is not always easy, nor is it always found. Crucial time is taken away from their most important task of meeting the artistic mission of their organization and absorbed by the fund-raising and development process.

Identifying Solutions

The Massachusetts Council on the Arts and Humanities sought ways to identify the main difficulties and possible solutions for development of affordable space for artists and cultural facilities. What were the major stumbling blocks? Where were the solutions? What were appropriate roles for the Council to take? To answer these questions, a series of research studies were conducted by a consortium of artists involved in development of studio space, graduate students of the Kennedy School of Government at Harvard University, and experts in development and finance. This research surveyed artists; analyzed models of development from artists associations, community development corporations, and private developers; and evaluated the potential role of federal, state, local, nonprofit, and private sources of financing.

The extent of the crisis was represented by the results of a Council-sponsored survey of 3,000 visual artists conducted by Friends of Boston Art. The artists' responses indicated that 21% did not have a studio, 59% were seeking space or expected to do so in the coming year, and 46% were under the threat of displacement from their current work space.[10] Subsequent research on behalf of cultural organizations and artists uncovered the following needs and concerns:

• Affordable, appropriate space stable over the long term

- Perceptions of artists by financial institutions, local and state government, and community groups
- Expanded access to state development finance programs
- Need for expertise in property management and leasing
- Lack of information and technical assistance on available buildings, financing mechanisms, and the development process

In response, the Council created The Space Program to provide technical and financial assistance to increase the amount of affordable space for artists and cultural organizations. The Space Program included several components:

- Expert technical advisors in the areas of development and finance who were available for free, informal, short-term consultations
- Grants for technical studies required prior to the development of cultural facilities
- Revolving Loan Fund for development of artists housing in partnership with another state organization, the Community Economic Development Assistance Corporation
- Tools to educate community and financial leaders on the development of artists' housing and studio space

Working through the Maze of Development and Finance

For many artists and cultural organizations, the most overwhelming need is technical assistance in the early stage of the development process. They require help in comprehending the new maze of language and regulations in the development process, communicating with real estate experts, understanding the financial options available, and figuring out the tasks required to accomplish their goals. Often, artists and cultural organizations are in a quandary just trying to identify their space needs and articulate their concerns.

The Space Program responded most effectively by providing experienced development and finance consultants who could sit down one on one with artists or cultural organizations. Some of their needs were met by a single consultation with a technical advisor, others required extensive meetings and counseling. The most typical requests for assistance included a need to:

- Locate appropriate space for their work
- Determine the financial feasibility of purchasing or renovating a facility
- Negotiate with property owners
- Understand and comply with legal and regulatory procedures, such as zoning, permits, and other requirements
- Secure financial assistance for the early, predevelopment stages of a project, in addition to construction and permanent financing

This technical advice was extremely important in the early stages of development. Help from experts familiar with the unique physical requirements of artists' housing/studio space and cultural facilities expedited the complex process of real estate development for the groups requesting assistance. Lessons learned from this approach would be extremely useful for other efforts.

The advantages of this relatively informal approach to technical assistance are a quick turn-around time, flexibility, the elimination of extensive application forms, and the reliance on excellent development experts and their positive individual relationships with artists and cultural organizations. Often the consultants put organizations that were facing similar problems in touch with each other. Frequently, the need for assistance was more intensive, however, and outside technical advice was required.

PROVIDING DEVELOPMENT EXPERTISE TO ARTISTS
AND CULTURAL ORGANIZATIONS ON AN
INFORMAL, ONE-ON-ONE BASIS WAS ONE OF THE
MOST USEFUL ASPECTS OF OUR PROGRAM.

Funds for Cultural Facilities

The requests for assistance to The Space Program confirmed the assumption that the earliest stage of the development process is the most difficult to evaluate and to fund. Without extensive knowledge or studies, how can you analyze the feasibility of a project? Most artists and cultural organizations have little development expertise and few funds for technical analysis. How can a bank be convinced that the proposed project is sound if the applicants have limited development experience and no impressive design plans or market or financial analyses to submit? The proponents themselves must be convinced of the viability of a project, which requires detailed financial review, engineering and design studies, and legal review.

The individual consultations with artists and cultural organizations described earlier were essential in the beginning stages of the development process, but detailed analyses were not possible on this basis. To meet this need, the Council established the Cultural Facilities Technical Assistance Program, which gave grants for development and technical consultants (such as architects, engineers, designers, and lawyers), zoning or variance fees, or other relevant costs necessary in the predevelopment stage of a project. Cultural organizations could target their own most pressing needs, identify the consultants with whom they wanted to work, and apply to the Council for funds to accomplish specific objectives. Examples of projects funded under this program included the following.

- The Boston Center for the Arts hired an architect to update the master plan for its complex of six historic buildings to include artists' galleries, studios, theater space, and offices.
- The Performing Arts School of Worcester conducted a feasibility study for renovation of its facility, which houses six nonprofit arts organizations.
- The Boston Ballet Company completed designs for a new building to house its rehearsal and performance space and its school.

The grant review process required application materials briefly justifying the need for the funds, the qualifications of the consultants to be hired by the cultural organization, and the proposed budget for the services. These grants were intended for the predevelopment stage of the projects; by state regulation they could not be used for capital construction.

Although the Massachusetts Council on the Arts and Humanities was restricted from financing construction of cultural facilities, staff worked to amend the legislation of the Massachusetts Industrial Finance Agency, which offers tax-exempt financing for projects with a stated public purpose. Even with the change in legislation, the finance agency did not generally approve artists' housing and cultural facility projects. Public awareness of this potential source of funds for cultural facility development was low, and few applications were submitted.

The Council worked with the Massachusetts Industrial Finance Agency to issue a research and market feasibility study of cultural facility financing issues and needs for the agency. This study revealed that over half of the respondents were in the predevelopment planning stages of cultural facility development, expansion, or renovation, and the average amount of financing required was $750,000.[11] Although the stated need for cultural facility development financing was extensive, the number of applications to eligible state agencies was surprisingly small. Many cultural organizations do not realize they are eligible for state assistance. More targeted outreach and education on the part of the cultural facilities as well as the public finance organizations was needed.

Most recently, the Massachusetts Cultural Council and the Massachusetts Industrial Finance Agency jointly established the Massachusetts Facilities Fund to aid nonprofit cultural organizations in the state. The Council provides funds for technical assistance related to cultural facility development, and $1.5 million is set aside for below-market loans or loan guarantees for the Facilities Fund.

Few states provide the resources and legislative mandate enabling state arts councils to award grants for *construction* of cultural facilities. The Illinois Arts Council was the first to begin such an initiative through the Build Illinois program; the funding came from the state's extensive transportation bonding allocation. Although this program was extremely short-lived, it established important precedents for development assistance for cultural facilities; the state now continues to offer technical assistance and educational workshops related to facility development. The New York State Council on the Arts also offered funds for rehabilitation of cultural facilities. This program emphasized renovation of facilities for handicapped accessibility, among other topics, and was noteworthy in that state arts council funds could be used for capital construction.

A more recent example currently in formation is the Cultural Facilities Fund, which was created as a project of the Nonprofit Facilities Fund in New York. Their recent National Cultural Facilities Study documented their survey of 93 cultural organizations and nonprofit leaders around the country, particularly those who had renovated or constructed new facilities. The major finding of this research was that "typical facilities projects sapped management and financial capacity, ultimately harming the artistic programs and undermining the long-term financial health of the organizations."[12]

The Cultural Facilities Fund was created to respond to this serious dilemma. Operating on a national and a local level, the Fund will create local programs to assist arts organizations in developing successful cultural facilities in their communities. Technical assistance, training, and information will be offered, in addition to loans and grants for cultural facilities. The crucial roles of advocacy and education in the field are also emphasized in this new initiative.

Educating the Financial Power Brokers

The most difficult obstacle for most artists in developing affordable living and working space is financing. Many banks and financial institutions have the misperception that artists are not serious workers or that they are not committed to repaying their mortgage loans. Lenders and public officials fear that artist enclaves would not be acceptable to communities or that neighbors would have reasons to object. One of the Council's first efforts at advocacy and education was targeted toward the financial leaders. Both public- and private-sector decision makers must understand the economic and community benefits of artists' housing development and cultural facilities.

SEEING ARTISTS' STUDIOS FIRST-HAND CHANGED
BANKERS' MISPERCEPTIONS ABOUT THE
FINANCIAL VIABILITY OF THESE DEVELOPMENTS.

To counteract these stereotypes and to educate the financial community, the Council sponsored a tour of successful artists' live/work developments in the Boston area for the officials of the state finance authorities and area banks. The tour was very successful in raising awareness of the importance and economic viability of these projects. Bankers realized the supreme dedication of the artists to their work and how that reflects in their commitment to the mortgage. Public agencies recognized the positive community impact of the artists' housing and studio space projects where neighborhoods were revitalized and stabilized. All were struck by the financial commitment of artists to their places of work. As one artist stated:

My studio is my livelihood. If I don't pay off my mortgage each month, I can't work. I'd rather give up on food than not pay my loan to the bank.

Direct observation and testimony are effective tools to educate lenders about the worth of a project, but it is not always possible to convince busy executives to take time out of their offices for a site visit. The Council decided to create a mechanism to bring the convincing projects directly to the financial power brokers instead.

Focusing on the target audience of public and private lenders and community leaders, the Council produced an eleven-minute video entitled *Creating Artists Space*. This effective video showed examples and images of successful artists' projects that were converted from former schools and industrial buildings. The video included testimony from artists, developers, community groups, neighbors, and public officials about the benefits of creating artists' studios and housing. The video, produced by Cambridge Studios, was shown to skeptical bankers, convincing them later to finance other artists' developments. *Creating Artists Space* received a Certificate for Creative Excellence from the International Awards Competition of the U.S. Industrial Film and Video Festival and was distributed nationally to help others successfully create affordable space for artists to live and work.

Creating Affordable Space for Artists

Although the Council helped artists with advocacy, education, and technical assistance, the agency did not have the legislative capability to provide long-term financial assistance. For this reason, the Council decided to contract with another state agency, the Massachusetts Community Economic Development Assistance Corporation (CEDAC), who had a proven track record, expertise, and commitment toward development of affordable housing. Through an interagency agreement, the Council allocated funds to CEDAC to create a Revolving Loan Fund for artists' housing and studio space. This partnership was the first time that Council funds were allocated to another state agency to establish a loan fund. This partnership was strategic because it combined the advantages of the arts council's commitment and contact with artists with the state development corporation's expertise, financing capabilities, and commitment to community revitalization and housing.

COMMITMENT TO THE ARTS CAN RESULT IN
AFFORDABLE HOUSING WHILE PROVIDING A
BOOST TO COMMUNITY DEVELOPMENT.

Three types of low-interest loans were available to non-profit groups. Site control loans provided a maximum of $42,500 to purchase an option on property or to make a down payment toward the purchase of privately owned property. Technical assistance loans provided up to $40,000 to help pay for the preliminary development and planning costs required for the renovation or construction of a property. Front money loans, up to $75,000 per request, helped finance such necessary items as the architectural, legal, engineering, project management, and other related development costs.

The Council's advisors to The Space Program typically would work with groups of artists to help them understand the development process. The artist organization would then be directed to CEDAC, who provided further technical assistance and guided the group through the agency's loan application process. All requests for funding were submitted to CEDAC's Board of Directors for approval.

Examples of projects funded through the Revolving Loan Fund included the Brickbottom Artists Project in Somerville near Boston, one of the largest artists' live/work space projects in the country, which was later featured in the videotape *Creating Artists Space*. The CEDAC loan was used for architectural expenses necessary to have the property appraised and surveyed. Another loan for architectural fees was issued to the Mission Hill Project, a proposed artists live/work cooperative in Boston. Both projects were complex and required substantial development expertise. The partnership with CEDAC and the technical advice provided by development consultants to the Council were important resources to the artists.

Brickbottom artists development

The fortitude of artists working together to create the Brickbottom development is worth further mention. Through extraordinary effort, a long-abandoned industrial building was developed into 85 units of affordable artists' housing/studio space, a cooperatively owned art gallery, and 60 units of market-rate condominiums. A group of 55 dedicated artists met weekly for three years to plan the artists cooperative. These artists unwittingly became experts in real estate development, finance, law, and politics through their struggles to make their dream of Brickbottom a reality.

Tired of being forced out of their studios as rents increased, the artists were dedicated to developing a community that would meet their artistic requirements as well as their need for an affordable, stable place to work and live. After an extensive search to find the best property to meet their needs, the artists agreed on a 250,000-square-foot warehouse located near an elevated highway in the middle of an industrial area. The Brickbottom Building, named after the bricks made in the building from local soil, lent itself well to artists' studios due to the twelve-foot high ceilings, steel-reinforced floors, large windows, and freight elevators.

The Brickbottom project was originally developed as a "limited equity cooperative" in which the artists' units would only be resold to other artists at a limited fixed rate of profit in order to keep the units affordable. The units on the upper floors were sold at market rate with no restrictions placed on their resale; these sales helped underwrite the cost of the artists' studios. After extensive debate, the artists later converted the limited-equity form of ownership to a condominium form of ownership. The $14 million project was financed by the artists' and condominium owners' equity, state loan guarantees, and private financing from area banks. This project is one of the largest artists' developments in the country, and it is certainly one of the most complex. This group of artists converted a stark industrial area into a small vibrant neighborhood full of activity, creativity, children, and art.

Combining Arts and Community

Implicit in the Brickbottom example and other programs presented in this chapter is the benefit of the arts and culture on the community. Artists' housing, cultural facilities, and artists themselves all contribute to the vitality of our cities and towns. An equally important side of the equation is the advantage to communities in working with the arts. These two groups working together, furthermore, can accomplish much more than each could individually.

The New England Foundation for the Arts, a regional consortium of arts agencies, decided to pursue opportunities for collaboration between arts and community development organizations. In partnership with the Massachusetts Association of Community Development Corporations, the Foundation convened a forum of leaders in the arts, community development, and foundations from throughout New England to ask tough questions of each other about ways in which these groups could better work together. The goals of the retreat, entitled *Broadening Our Vision: Connecting the Arts and Community Development,* were to explore opportunities for the arts and community-based groups to learn from each other, to identify leaders and organizations who could work together, and to uncover mechanisms to encourage future collaborations.

Similar to many of the partnerships described throughout this book, our first task was to define the terms and make sure each group understood the language and concerns of the other. At first glance, people in the arts and in community development view themselves as belonging to two very different worlds. As communication evolved, however, we found that the two groups fight many similar battles and share compatible goals and values. The major points of commonality include a continual need to:

- Define and reflect the community around us
- Fight battles for funding and our very existence
- Resolve conflicts among different ideas about the character of their neighborhood or our work
- Use creativity to find solutions to difficult problems
- Be politically savvy
- Adapt to change
- Express a vision for the future

As a tool to test possible struggles, approaches, and answers to partnerships between the arts and community development, we created three prototypical exercises for the conference participants. People were divided into teams and asked to solve one of three problems relating to the arts and downtown development, rural growth and change, or neighborhoods and cultural identity. The main questions posed in these three exercises, based on typical issues drawn from the region, included:

- *Arts and Economic Development* Can redevelopment of a vacant mill space or downtown storefronts serve as a catalyst for an older urban city while addressing the neighborhood and cultural needs?

- *Rural Community Growth, Change, and Identity* How can a small town best deal with issues of community growth and change while fostering the cultural life of the area?

- *Community Cultural Development Plan* How can a cultural center influence the redevelopment of its neighborhood and serve the community while meeting its own artistic mission?

Initially these exercises were difficult for the participants. Identifying the key issues in these situations required people to grasp complexities of community development, the arts, politics, business, and psychology. Devising answers to these questions was even harder, but the solutions suggested were extremely creative. The teams presented a full array of approaches, many incorporating community-based business enterprises, community cultural plans, involvement of neighborhood youth in job training and arts programs, and projects that support other cultural or neighborhood-based operations. Most importantly, the process of trying to solve these exercises in small groups enabled artists to understand how community developers did their job, while the people involved in community development were surprised at the lessons they could learn from artists.

Seeing models of successful collaborations brought tangible opportunities for partnership into focus. As part of the conference, a slide show was presented to illustrate examples of successful integration of arts and community from around the country. A few examples are highlighted below.

One Artist Row is an "arts incubator" developed by The Neighborhood Institute, a community development organization in Chicago. The arts incubator houses twenty-three studios, offices, and shops occupied by visual artists, entrepreneurs, and cultural organizations; it serves as a place to support and expand arts-related businesses and activities. Tenants receive technical assistance in business development and management through The Neighborhood Institute's Small Business Development Center. The success of this project led to development of a second arts incubator facility called Two Artist Row, which will offer office and rehearsal space as well as performance space that can be adapted to the changing needs of area organizations.

The Pittsburgh Cultural District stemmed from a master plan for revitalization of a fourteen-block area intended as a stimulus for economic development of the downtown area. This ambitious project is spearheaded by the Pittsburgh Cultural Trust, a nonprofit organization that works in close partnership with many key players, including the city, the county, and the Heinz Endowment. The Trust's first physical legacy was acquisition and restoration of an old movie theater into the 2800-seat Benedum Center for the Performing Arts, now used by many cultural groups in the region. Other critical accomplishments of this downtown revitalization include completion of the 32-story CNG Tower, the reopened 1300-seat Fulton Theater, riverfront area improvements, sidewalk renovations with amenities for pedestrians, commissioned public art, and a renewed faith in the future of downtown Pittsburgh.

The combination of art and community can occur on a much smaller, more intimate scale as well. One person can galvanize an entire community through art. Textile artist and community organizer Patryc Wiggins, for example, reflects the culture and history of her hometown of Newport, New Hampshire, through a large tapestry mural that she is weaving. The tapestry tells the story of Newport, home of the Dorr Mill, one of the few remaining woolen mills in New Hampshire. A

THE MASTER PLAN FOR THE PITTSBURGH CULTURAL DISTRICT SPURRED ECONOMIC REVITALIZATION OF THE DOWNTOWN.

third-generation Newport mill worker, Wiggins describes the goals of the tapestry project to highlight the heritage of the community, particularly the contributions of immigrants and women, to develop an understanding of the economic impact of industrialization on families, and to use art and history more effectively to address the community's chronic social problems.

Wiggins is working with the community through the schools and specially developed curriculum, collaborative programming through the town's cultural and civic organizations, public lectures, exhibits, a newsletter, artists' residencies, and an oral history project. Weekly Open Studios are held at the local library that sponsors this project by donating studio and office space and which serves as the umbrella organization for foundation support. The completed tapestry will be six feet by thirteen feet in size and will be permanently installed as the focal point in the main foyer of the new Sugar River Valley Technical Center in Newport. The impact of this project is perhaps best described by Wiggins' own words:

I feel that community development has to happen within the soul of the people and that is why art and education are vital tools for any meaningful community transformation.

DETAIL OF TAPESTRY DESIGN BY PATRYC WIGGINS, A THIRD-GENERATION MILL WORKER, ARTIST, AND COMMUNITY ORGANIZER, WHO DEMONSTRATES HOW MUCH IMPACT ONE INDIVIDUAL CAN HAVE.

Stories such as the ones described above provide important inspiration and models for change. An outgrowth of this conference was a commitment by the two sponsoring organizations to create funding programs related to arts and community development. In addition, the retreat served as a catalyst for specific partnerships between arts groups and community development groups. The program plan for this new initiative includes creation of an advisory or resource component, long-term funding, advocacy, and education. The process is ongoing.

Throughout the discussions of arts and community development, the need for support from government and financing organizations was emphasized. Real estate development costs money, and many projects are eligible for assistance from state or local government sources. The next chapter explores an unusual approach for getting the attention and the mandate with public finance and development agencies to focus on the impact of their public dollars on the design and character of your neighborhood.

Chapter 6

INTEGRATING DESIGN INTO FINANCE AND DEVELOPMENT

In advocating for quality design, the most effective places to target are the organizations and institutions with the *power*, *mandate*, and *resources* to create buildings and public places. In government, look to the development and finance agencies and authorities. As summarized in the window titled "Who Affects Design?" in Chapter 1, the key players in the public design and development process are the housing and development authorities, public works departments, highway and transportation agencies, and the financing authorities who control funds for public and/or private development. You will find the resources, power, and opportunity in these organizations. Where else can you find the legislative mandate and the funding to affect an entire city or state? If you work for one of these agencies, or if you can leverage influence over someone who does, then you can play a powerful role in improving the design and development of our publicly built environment.

Design Implications for Finance and Development Agencies

Most public agencies responsible for finance or development guard their mission very diligently. They make sure that projects under their review are financially feasible, meet certain public policy goals, and follow special requirements and procedures. Although these agencies typically have a long list of regulations to approve, they generally do not consider the *design* implications of their mandate. These agencies do not generally have designers on their staff or boards, nor do issues of design typically arise during funding or policy discussions. When agencies do consider the issue of design effectively, however, the benefits are far-reaching. Development and finance agencies have the leverage and resources to make a difference on a very large scale. If managed properly, attention to design quality will continue throughout subsequent governmental administrations and become part of the institutional ethic, memory, and ongoing practices of the agency.

In looking for an opportunity to make a difference the Massachusetts Council on the Arts and Humanities recognized the untapped opportunity with the approximately twenty state agencies and authorities responsible for finance and development. These agencies spend an estimated *$2.2 billion each year* constructing, renovating, or financing public facilities such as schools, hospitals, public institutions, parks, and highways. Yet the mandate for many of these agencies did not include consideration of design. By educating state finance and development agencies about the impact of their projects on communities, an unimaginable opportunity for design advocacy unfolds.

Creating State Design Policy for Long-Term Change

In order to increase our impact and legitimacy with the state agencies, the Council formed a partnership with the Secretary of the Executive Office of Administration and Finance, Frank

Keefe, who formerly served as director of the Office of State Planning and was keenly committed to quality design and development. Critical to our initiative, the Executive Office of Administration and Finance controlled the budgets of many of the agencies we wanted to influence.

In exploring ways to improve public development in the state, Keefe suggested that he issue a call for action through an "Administrative Bulletin," which is a governmental mechanism that directs agencies to follow certain procedures or to establish regulations to accomplish specific goals. As ultimately issued, Administrative Bulletin #88-5, "State Policies on Design," directed state development and finance agencies to create and implement policies on design that would influence the way they financed or constructed projects in the Commonwealth. As stated in the Administrative Bulletin, agencies were encouraged to operate their policies on three levels:

1. Requiring consideration of design quality through agency *procedures*
2. Providing *incentives* that encourage and/or reward design quality
3. Promoting increased understanding of design issues through *education* and *communication*

Our goal was *not* to turn these agencies into "design czars" or to have staff tell architects what color brick to use in a building. Rather, our hope was that design would be raised as an important concern at the bargaining table or, ideally, *before* projects got to the bargaining table. If an agency felt that a project deserved financing on public policy or financial feasibility terms but that it had serious design flaws, for example, the applicant would be asked to improve the design of the proposed development. The staff of the agencies would be aware of design issues, but they were not expected to be experts. They would have access to design expertise when needed.

OUR INTENT WAS NOT TO TURN STATE AGENCIES INTO "DESIGN CZARS" BUT RATHER TO RAISE DESIGN AS AN ISSUE *PRIOR* TO THE APPROVAL OF PUBLIC FUNDS.

Applicants to state development and finance programs would be advised at the earliest stage that design is a factor in the agencies' criteria for allocation of public dollars. It is not fair to developers or project proponents to raise the criteria of quality design *after* they have jumped through the many hoops of project review and have already completed their designs. The message to be emphasized is that the state has high standards for design and development of the projects that it funds, and applicants for state financing or contracts should raise their standards and expectations as well. As Frank Keefe stated:

We should ask state agencies that regulate and develop to think about programming, design policy, and instruction up front and in an integrated fashion.

Drafting the Administrative Bulletin

The actual drafting of the Administrative Bulletin on Design Policy was not an easy task. We kept looking for models or precedents from other states or localities. None existed—so we created our own. The language of the bulletin was drafted and redrafted, with valuable assistance from planners, designers, and writers. The language ultimately used (and as shown in the exerpts of the bulletin given here) may be useful to other states or localities interested in adapting this mechanism for their communities.

Since the concept of state agency design policies was new, we wanted to provide the participating agencies with assistance on the types of policies they might consider and ways of implementing this order without causing undue bureaucratic delay or interference. The language of the Administrative Bulletin included suggested types of procedures, incentives, and educational opportunities possible for agencies to include in their state policies on design. As cited in the Administrative Bulletin, specific examples were presented, such as:

Procedures

- Include guidelines for selection of qualified designers.
- Establish mechanisms to improve coordination and communication among agencies involved in design, development, and financing of projects.

Incentives

- Provide financial incentives for design quality.
- Cooperate with other state agencies to establish a "Design Facilitation Team" using designers from various state agencies who have been trained to consult with agencies on a periodic basis.

Educational Opportunities

- Emphasize design quality in all agency publications and written procedures or manuals.
- Include language about design quality in all contracts authorizing construction projects.
- Train staff about design and development issues.

Putting the Program into Action: Educating the Leadership

The first step in implementing the Administrative Bulletin was to raise agency directors' understanding of the significance of design to their day-to-day operations. Some agencies, particularly the housing authority and the agencies responsible for communities and development, were already actively involved in design. The agencies responsible for finance, however, were not used to operating with design as a criteria for funding, and therefore they required a higher degree of advocacy and education.

We targeted approximately twenty state development and finance agencies. Each director was invited to attend a day-long retreat on design and to bring one chief assistant. We were well aware that the actual crafting of each state agency's design policy would most likely be undertaken by a staff member rather than the director. Involving the key staff person along with the executive director was an important strategic decision.

GOOD DESIGN CANNOT SIMPLY BE
LEGISLATED OR MANDATED. COMMITMENT
TO QUALITY DESIGN MUST BE DIRECTED FROM
THE LEADERSHIP AT THE VERY TOP.

Perhaps the hardest task in planning this retreat was convincing these busy development and finance directors that they should take a day out of their schedule to talk about design. The retreat was planned intentionally to be a day away from the hectic demands of running a state agency to focus on the Administrative Bulletin and design. Getting the *directors'* attention was crucial. Commitment to quality design from the leadership makes the difference and filters down throughout the organization. Without the directors involved, implementation of the Administrative Bulletin would not be feasible.

The day before the workshop was to occur, it became clear that many directors were sending middle-level managers instead of attending personally. For that reason, the Secretary of the Office of Administration and Finance canceled the workshop. The main goal of educating the leadership could not be met if all the agency directors did not attend. We then regrouped and asked the directors to take a more active role in the planning of the workshop and to participate in presentations at the rescheduled event. Involving the directors in this stage was valuable in making them more committed to the success of this initiative.

The workshops provided the participants with a basic understanding of design concepts and terminology, a forum for discussion of their organization's role in the design process, and a chance to test ideas to be included in their state agency design policies. The first workshop, entitled "Public Agencies as the Catalyst of Good Design," served as an overview on design issues and how they relate to the agencies' mandate. Many of the directors admitted that participating in the panels forced them to assess for the first time the actual impact of design on their agency's mandate and to learn firsthand just how their organization met or fell short of that challenge.

The importrance of the workshop was perhaps best stated by the keynote speaker, Mayor John Bullard of New Bedford, Massachusetts:

On the local level, communities must live with the consequences of whatever design processes exist at the state and federal level. The designers and bureaucrats come and go, but the structure forever becomes part of the landscape.

Due to the success of the first retreat, the Council and the Executive Office of Administration and Finance decided to cosponsor a second workshop which focused on the drafting and implementation of the agencies' response to the Administrative Bulletin. The second retreat included panels on topics such as "Public Design Makes a Difference," "Growth, Development, and Design Quality," and "Creating a Design Policy." Working groups were established to help the agencies respond to the Administrative Bulletin. The types of questions covered in the group discussions, which are important for any public agency to explore, included:

- At what level in your agency are decisions made and actions taken that influence design quality?
- Given the mandate of your agency and the larger development issues discussed today, what policies might you create to help ensure design quality?
- In creating policies on design, what management and implementation strategies would you include?
- What policies or actions would you suggest for more effective coordination among state agencies?

The level of discussion and interest in the workshop debates was extraordinary. Participants' comments included the following:

We must continue to create forums for communication. We need a learning system to understand what others are doing. Each agency should draft a mission statement that establishes its goals.
TUNNEY LEE, AGENCY DIRECTOR, DIVISION OF CAPITAL PLANNING AND OPERATIONS

We live in a world today where the public realm is designed by various experts in different fields who never talk to each other and by financial entities. All these forces collide randomly, and whatever results is what we call our public world.
ROBERT CAMPBELL, ARCHITECTURE CRITIC AND SPEAKER

We should focus on design quality and process as well as on cost and time. Encourage public comment and participation before the project becomes a fait accompli.
CONFERENCE PARTICIPANT

Proceedings from the two retreats were compiled and distributed to all relevant state agencies in order to share the ideas generated at the sessions. Several agency directors said it was one of their most rewarding days in state government.

The second retreat provided a forum for agencies with similar concerns and missions to work together on their policies. Experts in development, design, and public administration provided assistance on the types of policies and procedures that could be created as a response to the Administrative Bulletin. The technical assistance was in the form of one-on-one meetings, outside experts meeting with small working groups, and review of design policies by representatives of the Boston Society of Architects as well as Council staff.

An added benefit of the workshops, according to agency directors, was the opportunity to meet with other directors to discuss issues of mutual concern. The directors were able to solve interagency problems or development controversies in the context of conversations about design and the Administrative Bulletin.

While the success of the retreats was self-evident, the long-term impact was undocumented initially. We were rewarded several months later, however, when the following comment was received from the town planner of Franklin, Massachusetts:

I had been struggling with an architect from the MBTA about a train station they were building in our downtown. Every time I complained about the design, he insisted it was fine, and I had no reason to request an improvement. Finally I gave up. Several months later he came back to me with a new, much improved, and elegant design. When I asked him what made him change his mind, he responded, "Well, the Chairman of the MBTA went to this conference on design, and he came back and insisted that we all work a lot harder on the design of our stations. That really made a difference!"

Developing Policies on Design

After capturing the attention of the directors at the retreats, we wanted to be sure they created public policies that advanced design quality through day-to-day agency operations. Although the current leadership of the organizations recognized the benefits of design, that concern would not necessarily carry through in the inevitable turnover of government leadership and staff. To the greatest extent possible, we wanted to "institutionalize" a concern for quality design. We wanted agencies to establish procedures and a working style that would foster better public design. To guide the agencies in meeting these goals, the Administrative Bulletin listed characteristics necessary for implementation of the design policies. As stated in the Administrative Bulletin:

AN ACCEPTABLE POLICY MUST:

- Work toward improvement of design quality of the Commonwealth.

- Include a detailed implementation plan which allocates responsibility for tasks and details a time line for implementation and review.

- Be implemented with little or no additional cost or bureaucratic delay to the agency.

- Have a built-in review process which ensures evaluation of the effects and effectiveness of the policy.

- Have a built-in mechanism which requires coordination among agencies working on the same or related projects.

As agency staff worked to draft their policies, we set up working groups to bring together agencies with similar missions or mandates. Technical expertise was provided by senior staff members of the most experienced agencies, the Council, and volunteer members of the Boston Society of Architects. We held special meetings with the agencies' legal counsels to ensure that the Administrative Bulletin did not conflict with any existing regulations. Summaries of all the participating agencies' policies were distributed to all twenty state development and finance agencies.

Throughout this effort, we were clearly aware that good design cannot simply be legislated or mandated. Our motive in seeking administrative or procedural change was to encourage state agencies to establish an organizational structure, proper incentives, administrative procedures, appropriate guidelines, and positive examples that enable good design to occur. Just because a law or a procedure is on the books, there is no assurance that future leadership will continue its implementation. The longer a legacy exists of projects that cause citizens and public employees to be proud, the greater the likelihood that the tradition will continue.

Results of the Administrative Bulletin on Design

What were the major results of this initiative? State agency staff members who rarely heard the word *design* uttered in the hallways struggled long and hard to create their state policies on design. Other agencies that had a successful history of design found ways to share their experience with others. Some agencies used design for the first time as one of several funding criteria; other agencies ignored the directive.

The written product varied as well. A couple of agencies compiled reams of information into a document as their response to the Administrative Bulletin, thus making it unwieldy and difficult to digest. Perhaps the best response came from the Community Economic Development Assistance Corporation, which submitted a one-page, elegantly written document that integrated the goals of the program. Summaries of the design policies created by each agency as a response to the Administrative Bulletin are presented in the accompanying window. The real results of this project will be determined several years from now as a legacy of quality design and development is created.

Benefits to the state

Adoption of formal design policies as a result of Administrative Bulletin #88-5 provided agencies with an opportunity to consolidate and rethink existing procedures and create new procedures for their operations. The sessions created to help agencies respond to the Administrative Bulletin gave them a forum to discuss complex issues of mutual concern. Several agency directors stated that this program offered them an important and rare opportunity to meet with each other and to produce tangible results.

Highlights of selected state design policies are summarized below:

- Recognition of the importance of design quality for long-term financial success of the funded projects
- Addition of design quality as a criterion in the evaluation of applications for state funding

Summary of State Agencies' Policies on Design

Community Economic Development Assistance Corporation (CEDAC)

The policy statement recognizes that quality design makes the agency's loans more solid and "therefore, to advance CEDAC's mission and to reduce the risk associated with its lending, CEDAC will promote attention, concern, and responsiveness to the quality of design." In evaluating loans, CEDAC will include questions about design and the designer's qualifications, enable sufficient fees in development pro formas and financing to let the project benefit from design professionals, and assist developers by providing technical assistance in the selection of designers and in contracting for design services.

Department of Corrections

The Department of Corrections issued "Design, Development and Planning Guidelines," which established department policy concerning design for the planning, construction, and renovation of correctional institutions and facilities. The guidelines focus on technical standards, functional needs, health and safety standards, and efficiency. Guidelines also set standards for interior design and furnishings.

Division of Capital Planning and Operations (DCPO)

DCPO established incentives to encourage design firms to exceed the professional standards required in their contracts. Examples include a designer bonus program that offers a financial bonus to designers who exceed standard requirements in their work and a designer awards program to reward quality in state design. In addition, DCPO discusses design issues in regular meetings held with user agencies, established liaison groups with professional agencies such as the Boston Society of Architects, set competitive market fees to attract highly qualified professionals, and holds public community meetings to discuss the visual impact of a public project.

Executive Office of Environmental Affairs

This policy emphasizes specific elements that agency designs should consider, such as buffer areas, natural site characteristics, visual and access corridors, landscape design, and historical and design consistency. Through the agency's Department of Environmental Management, existing policies and procedures emphasize their work toward quality design, including setting of budgets, hiring project staff, selecting designers, specifying services in the design contract (including artists), and supervising the designer and the construction. Specific actions that they identified which would improve their work include more codification of policies and procedures, post-construction analyses, and more standardized details for design problems commonly encountered in state park development.

HEALTH AND EDUCATIONAL FACILITIES AUTHORITY (HEFA)

HEFA proposed design criteria such as addressing architectural barriers, the relationship of architectural standards to ideals of local communities, locations that provide ready access to transportation and that minimize impact on service delivery, and feasibility of demand and impact of location on the use of facilities. These design goals would be stated in the informational materials and programs the agency prepares, and they would also be part of discussions with institutions requesting financing.

MASSACHUSETTS BAY TRANSIT AUTHORITY (MBTA)

The policy of the MBTA summarized the design procedures of the authority, such as publishing and implementing manuals that give directions and guidelines on such design elements as rider orientation, maintenance, graphics, lighting, comfort, safety, and community support; developing programs that incorporate public art within and along the public transit lines; and establishing design-related criteria for the acquisition of new equipment, stations, and facilities and the selection of consultants.

MASSACHUSETTS BOARD OF LIBRARY COMMISSIONS

Library facilities are required to be sensitive to local conditions, support present and future programs of the library service, and use qualified designers. Design quality and planning is part of the evaluation process for approval of financing. The Board of Library Commissioners created an active public information program that advises on selection of architects, maintains a visual collection and a file of sample designer selection policies and program statements, and conducts a variety of educational programs on library design and development.

MASSACHUSETTS DEPARTMENT OF PUBLIC WORKS

The Department of Public Works' policy emphasizes their role as designers, builders, and maintainers of the "streets, roads, and highways which are the setting for homes, shops, businesses, and public institutions." Their design policy outlined a number of organizational changes, including (1) identification of a continuous project manager for all phases of development; (2) use of a project description to guide project development and to serve as a gauge of success, rather than relying solely on quantitative definitions and goals; (3) using design quality as one basis of hiring and promotion; (4) revision of the *Highway Design Manual*; (5) and more vigorous consultant monitoring. In addition, special efforts were cited, such as the Open Space Program, the Landscape Section, and the Beautification Project.

MASSACHUSETTS HOUSING AND FINANCE AGENCY (MHFA)

The existing general approaches to encouraging design excellence are included in MHFA's policy. The agency's policies are communicated to clients and to the public by highlighting successful projects, sending design guideline recommendations to developers and architects, and maintaining liaison with professional design societies. Quality design is an important criterion in the competitive process used to select developments for MHFA financing. A threshold design score must be reached. Finally, construction and operation of housing and post-occupancy evaluation are monitored by MHFA to provide continuous feedback in order to improve future housing.

MASSACHUSETTS PORT AUTHORITY (MASSPORT)

The design goals of Massport are defined in their policy: creation of facilities that are safe, modern, aesthetically pleasing, convenient, and efficient; encouraging innovation that minimizes adverse impacts on the neighboring communities; incorporation of artwork. To support these goals, Massport created designer selection procedures, awards contracts on the basis of evaluation by a Massport Designer Selection Board, and emphasizes design criteria in the selection of consultants. In addition, Massport continues to establish design guidelines for major facility projects, as well as for signs and graphics, and they include public art in development projects.

MASSACHUSETTS THRIFT FUND

The policy of the Thrift Fund states the agency's intent to incorporate design review in financial analysis by staff or through the assistance of professional design organizations. Projects deemed "patently detrimental to [their] environment or insensitive to [their] surroundings" will not be approved for financial assistance. Developers and designers of successful projects would be encouraged to reapply for similar efforts. The agency's interest in design awareness would be emphasized in agency publications and documents, which would set an appropriate tone by maintaining high graphic standards.

- Adoption of general design guidelines
- Updating design guidelines based on recent experience, using such tools as post-occupancy studies, post-construction evaluations, and life-cycle cost analysis
- Consultation with the Boston Society of Architects when relevant design expertise is not available in house
- Inclusion of public art
- Refinement of consultant selection procedures
- Use of high-quality graphics in agency publications and buildings

The agencies' design policies reflect the range of solutions and the potential benefit to the state. The process for education, advocacy, and technical assistance in creation of the Administrative Bulletin for Design Policies can be adapted to meet the needs of your locality and state. The most important ally is dedicated leadership to accomplish these goals.

Chapter 7

REWARDING QUALITY DESIGN: THE GOVERNOR'S DESIGN AWARDS PROGRAM

Capturing the Public's Attention

How can you capture the attention of the public, provide recognition to all the key actors in the development process, and provide education and awareness about the importance of design—in one program? The Governor's Design Awards Program accomplished these goals, and the process used in Massachusetts could be adapted and implemented in your state or locality.

Awards programs are successful mechanisms to recognize and encourage the best in design. Often private- or public-sector organizations or professional design organizations sponsor awards programs to identify the top talent in their field, to encourage others to strive for the best, and to provide positive exposure to the sponsor's mandate or product.

When working on a project, most designers or sponsors don't consciously think "I'll try a little harder so I can win this big award." Recognizing stellar accomplishment is a bonus for those who succeed and an incentive for others to try harder. Some sponsors may see awards and recognition as strategies for getting better products or public spaces from their designers.

Regardless of the initial incentive, public awareness and recognition of quality design serve as powerful advocacy tools for better design. The benefits are expanded considerably when awards programs recognize all the key participants in the design process and when citizens are involved.

Goals of the Governor's Design Awards Program

When the Governor's Design Awards Program was created, countless design awards programs existed. Not one, however, recognized all the major players in the design process, encouraged active citizen participation and public education, and involved site review by the design juries. The Massachusetts Council on the Arts and Humanities sponsored the first Governor's Design Awards Program in the country to include these components. The goal of the program was to spark public discussion about the significance of good design and to underscore the state's dedication to quality in its built environment. In addition, we wanted to increase the public's perception of the state's commitment to quality design.[13]

The Governor's Design Awards Program, sponsored by the Council and the Boston Society of Architects, recognized excellence in architecture, landscape architecture, urban design, and public improvements. This program was funded by a grant from the National Endowment for the Arts and by the Council over a two-year period. Before applying for funds we spent a year researching various approaches to public education and awards programs. Numerous awards programs existed in the design and artistic fields, but none had the citizen participation element we were seeking. We finally identified a successful program in England, the Civic Trust Awards Program, which was based on regional juries that held on-site evaluations of projects. We added the concept of on-site jury evaluations to our notion of intensive public outreach and education.

Citizens of the state were invited to nominate their favorite projects as candidates for a Governor's Design Award. Designers and developers were able to nominate their own projects as well. Awards were given not only to the designers of winning projects but also to other key participants. Both public-

and private-sector projects were eligible. Depending on the project, essential players such as the client, developer, financial backer, architect, engineer, landscape architect, or community group received an award. Public awards ceremonies were held throughout the state, and press coverage was extensive. Such characteristics made the Governor's Design Awards Program unique.

Implementing the Program

The Council issued a Request for Proposals to select a contractor to help implement the Governor's Design Awards Program. Through a very competitive process, the Council selected the Laboratory for Architecture and Planning at the Massachusetts Institute of Technology to administer the program. Mary Jane Daly, a city planner, was the very capable project director. We both worked very intensely developing and implementing this program; neither of us had ever worked harder on a program, nor had as much fun.

Finding creative ways to reach out to the public took substantial effort, but that element was essential to the success of this program. To increase our ability for outreach, we divided the state into five regions. In each region we appointed a five-person Regional Advisory Panel, typically comprised of an architect, a landscape architect, a planner, a leader in the business community, and a member of the media. The Regional Advisory Panels helped us to become more involved in each community, to announce the program more effectively, and to plan the regional awards ceremonies. These panels had no voting power in the selection of winning projects; that responsibility was given to separate Regional Design Juries.

The Regional Design Juries were responsible for selecting the winning projects in the first round of competition. Each five-person Design Jury was composed of a separate group of experts, including an architect, a landscape architect, a city planner, a person knowledgeable about historic preservation, and a member of the Regional Advisory Panel.

The Governor's Design Awards Program was two-tiered. Each region selected regional finalists. These finalists were then asked to submit presentation boards to be considered for a state-level award. A separate state-level design jury, comprised of five nationally known experts in architecture, planning, landscape architecture, and engineering, would select the statewide winners of the Governor's Design Awards Program.

Since a primary goal of the Governor's Design Awards Program was public awareness about design, extensive outreach was essential. Ten thousand well-designed posters announcing the Call for Nominations, including a postcard nomination form, were mailed out. Posters were sent to every city and town in the state. Every library, museum, arts and humanities organization, chamber of commerce, professional design association, newspaper, and radio or television station received a notice. In addition, we provided newspapers with special entry forms that many of them published so that their readers could submit entries. Some newspapers designed their own forms. We also gave many radio, newspaper, and television interviews to increase the media's attention to this project.

The intense public interest in design of their environment is indicated by the incredible response to our Call for Nominations. In less than six weeks 675 postcards were received from citizens across the state, nominating their favorite design project. Nominations came from a vast array of people: citizens, 4-H Clubs, designers, developers, public agencies, mayors, and residents of well-designed buildings. Entry forms required a minimal amount of information: the name and location of the design project, the nominator's name and address, and the name of the designer, if known. Nominators had the option of stating their reasons for selecting a project; almost all chose to respond.

We received some wonderful testimonies for projects, which often had the tone of "I like the project on Main Street next door to the post office. I don't know who designed it, but it always makes me feel special when I enter it." We had a staff of interns sleuthing to identify the designers of many of the places nominated so that we could contact the designers for the next stage of the competition. In addition to the entry forms, favorite projects were described in letters, postcards, greeting cards, drawings, and photographs. The nominations provided intriguing insight into the way this program captured the public's imagination and revealed people's real concern for places where they live, work, and play.

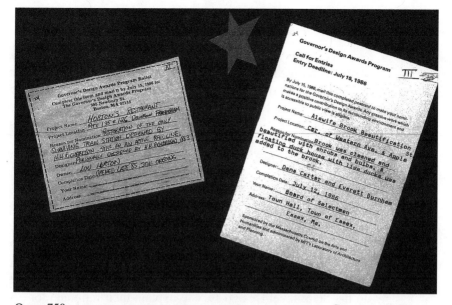

OVER 750 CITIZENS NOMINATED THEIR FAVORITE PLACES FOR A GOVERNOR'S DESIGN
AWARD, INDICATING THE EXTENT OF PUBLIC AWARENESS ABOUT DESIGN. (REPRINTED WITH
PERMISSION FROM THE MASSACHUSETTS CULTURAL COUNCIL.)

The Judging Process

Nominees for a Governor's Design Award were asked to prepare standard submission binders for review by the Regional
Design Juries. Required materials included a project credit
sheet, signed by both the designer and the client and listing all
the key participants in this project who would receive an award
if their project was selected; a two-page written designer's
statement; and various visual materials, such as slides. Over the
course of two months, the juries visited selected projects where
they spoke with users in preparation for selection of regional
winners. Although any architectural design, landscape design,
or public improvement was eligible for award, categories were
eschewed. Special mentions were established for projects that
did not meet the award criteria but that deserved recognition
for a special aspect, such as intent, impact, creative use of resources, or collaborative effort.

　　　The main criteria as listed in the Call for Entries stated the
goal very simply:

Winning projects must be comprehensively beneficial to their users, viewers, and the surrounding built and natural environment.

The jurors and the entrants were advised that submissions would be judged on their content and quality. Neither the scale and complexity of the project nor elaborate presentations were to affect jury decisions. Also guiding jury evaluations was the statement of the Governor's Design Awards Program "to recognize design that is more than stylish aesthetics."

The Design Juries evaluated all the submissions, conducted on-site evaluations of the top-ranked projects, and from that group selected the winners of regional awards. The regional winners were then asked to submit one presentation board which was to be the basis for review by the national design jury for the state-level awards. This jury did not make site visits, but they did review slides and the presentation materials. A member of the Regional Design Jury also made a presentation to the State-level Design Jury to explain their rationale for selection of the regional winners.

Awards were made at five regional ceremonies around the state. At the ceremonies standing room only prevailed. At each ceremony the regional jury presented the winning projects in a slide show and explained eloquently and directly the reasons for their decisions. After the slide shows presenting all the regional winners, the state-level jury gave their rationale for the winners of the second stage of the competition. Governor and Mrs. Michael Dukakis presented these state-level winners with their certificates at a special public ceremony, culminating the Governor's Design Awards Program.

The winning projects were then featured in an exhibition that traveled around the state. It consisted simply of framing of the winning exhibition boards along with an introductory panel. Exhibition sites were selected at well-designed places that were extremely accessible to the public, such as Heritage State Parks around the state (visited by thousands of tourists and residents each year), Logan International Airport, the Boston Public Library, and the annual trade association meeting of the Boston Society of Architects, known as "Build Boston," which approximately 8,500 people attend. A catalog documenting the program and the winning projects was distributed throughout the state and the country.

In addition to rewarding excellence in design, equally important goals of the program were to raise public awareness

THE CATALOG OF WINNING PROJECTS WAS AN IMPORTANT TOOL FOR WIDESPREAD PUBLIC EDUCATION ABOUT COMMUNITY DESIGN. (REPRINTED WITH PERMISSION FROM THE MASSACHUSETTS CULTURAL COUNCIL.)

about the significance of quality design in their communities and to underscore the state's commitment to quality design. These goals were met with a success that exceeded all expectations.

Diversity in Success

The diversity of submissions and winning projects is perhaps one of the most fascinating aspects of this project. Winning projects represent all parts of the Commonwealth and include diverse types of design. Just a sampling of winning projects includes congregate housing for the elderly, a downtown historic district, a wastewater treatment plant, a shelter for homeless men, a bridge, a park reclaimed from toxic wasteland, and a ventilation shaft connected to a subway station. This remarkable diversity of scale and use shares a common aspiration for excellence and represents the opportunities all around us for stellar design.

Comments from design jurors on some of the winning projects included:

HOLYOKE'S HERITAGE STATE PARK IS ONE OF SEVERAL HERITAGE PARKS THAT WON A GOVERNOR'S DESIGN AWARD. (REPRINTED WITH PERMISSION FROM THE MASSACHUSETTS CULTURAL COUNCIL.)

> *The Heritage State Park Program is creating a statewide system of urban places with consistently high standards of design and care. It has chosen hard problems, difficult sites, and complex physical and political settings. It has revealed our past in telling ways. It has sparked new investment. And it rewards all who care about place and history.*
>
> JOHN DE MONCHAUX, JURY CHAIR

> *The Mystic River Preservation Project represents a new generation of parks that have been created from toxic wasteland. Such an effort requires more than vision; it calls for new technologies of tremendous scope . . . this is an entirely new landscape representing the marriage of art and science in landscape architecture.*

> *Arts on the Line is commendable for the quality, diversity, and accessibility of the twenty site-specific art works chosen for its four stations. Projects like this don't just happen . . . this program attests to the value of taking risks to bring fine art to everyone.*
>
> SUSAN FREY, STATE JUROR

> *What we saw as being most positive about The Bridge of Flowers was that such a limited gesture, in terms of design energy, could*

CONVERSION OF THIS BUILDING ON CAPE COD INTO CONGREGATE HOUSING FOR THE EL-
DERLY WON A GOVERNOR'S DESIGN AWARD. (REPRINTED WITH PERMISSION FROM THE
MASSACHUSETTS CULTURAL COUNCIL.)

*have such a major impact. The kind of communal effort that was put
into it was impressive. It has a special spirit.*
RICHARD TREMAGLIO, REGIONAL JUROR

*The Yarmouth Street Ventilation Shaft has grace and humor as op-
posed to being an engineering solution to an engineering problem.*
BERNARD SPRING, STATE JUROR

Almost sixty projects around the state received Regional
Governor's Design Awards. Of that group, twelve received a
State-level Governor's Design Award and two received a Special Mention. The winning state-level projects are listed in the
accompanying table.

The most important elements to the success of this program were the quality of the design jurors, the jurors' site
visits, a dedicated staff, the public notification of the project,
and the workshops and exhibitions that occurred throughout
the state. This program can be replicated in any state, locality,
or region. It is important to underscore the public participation
in the program and the need to recognize *all* the key players in
the design process.

Governor's Design Awards Program
State-Level Winners

Project	Client and Developer	Designer
Massachusetts Heritage Parks Program	Executive Office of Environmental Affairs	Eight sites with separate state designers
Columbus Center Use Project, Springfield	Springfield Parking Authority	Cannon Design Mixed-Ramp Engineering
Lowell Heritage State Park, entrance plazas	Executive Office of Environmental Affairs	Carr, Lynch Associates
Construction fence mural 176 Federal Street, Boston	Centros Real Estate	Cvijanovic, Gropman, Judelson, Genereux, Gropman, Mumford
Faneuil Hall Marketplace, Boston	Boston Redevelopment Authority; The Rouse Company	Benjamin Thompson and Associates
Arts on the Line, Public Art in Transit Stations, Cambridge and Somerville	Executive Office of Transportation and Construction	Cambridge Arts Council and artists for twenty sites
MBTA Southwest Corridor, Yarmouth Street, Boston, ventilation shaft	Massachusetts Bay Transportation Authority	Stull and Lee, Inc.; Kaiser/Fay Spofford and Thorndike Engineers
Mystic River Reservation Park, Medford and Somerville	Metropolitan District Commission	Carol R. Johnson Associates; Pine and Swallow
St. John of Damascus Church, Dedham	St. John of Damascus Church	Imre and Anthony Halasz, Inc.
Captain Eldridge House, congregate housing for the elderly, Hyannis	Barnstable Housing Authority	Donham and Sweeney; KJA Architects
Nauticus Marina, Inc.	Nauticus Marina, Inc.	Studio for Osterville Architecture
Waterfront Historic Area League (WHALE), New Bedford	City of New Bedford	Waterfront Historic Area League

Special Mention Projects

Project	Client and Developer	Designer
John C. Nutting Apartments for Severely Disabled, Amherst	Amherst Housing Authority	Juster Pope Associates
The Bridge of Flowers, Shelburne Falls	Shelburne Falls Fire District; Town of Shelburne; Town of Buckland; Bridge of Flowers, Inc.	Community Effort; Dufresne-Henry, Inc.

Chapter 8

EDUCATION AS ADVOCACY: FROM PUBLIC OFFICIALS TO CHILDREN

No matter who you talk to—mayors, public officials, volunteer community boards, citizen activists, children—the needs expressed most urgently in improving their neighborhoods are *education* and *technical assistance.* Not even the ever-present demand for funds is expressed more forcefully. Often people in positions to influence change volunteer their time, but they do not have extensive expertise or resources to identify solutions. People yearn for good examples, successful lessons from others, and tips for making a difference in their communities.

For most of us, the very language of design and development can be overwhelming and confusing. We are intimidated by the notion of drawing or building things. This conflict is particularly ironic given every child's eagerness to pick up a crayon or build a complex tower out of blocks.

This chapter addresses education at the two most important levels for advocacy: *public leaders* who currently make the decisions affecting our built environment and *children* who will soon become the leaders or active citizens who can change the world around us.

Educating Public Leaders

In developing the Design and Development Program at the Massachusetts Council on the Arts and Humanities, we tapped experts in every field imaginable to solicit their insight into what was needed most to improve community design quality. Virtually every conversation emphasized the continual need for education and technical assistance. Our expectation was that people would complain the loudest about lack of resources; we did not anticipate their desire for information and successful examples.

For these reasons, and to fill an important gap in the field, the Council decided to produce a primer with related public workshops to help communities learn about the basic issues and language of community design. The book was designed to be a lively manual about the principles and consequences of design and planning to help citizens participate more effectively. The goal of this initiative was not to train people to become experts in design or to think that the solutions are easily obtainable by reading one book. Rather, the intent was to help them understand the relevant design issues and implications of certain actions, to know the correct questions to ask, to have more confidence to trust their own opinions, and to understand when help is needed.

The Council appointed an Advisory Board composed of designers, planners, and citizen activists to provide input to the project and to keep the standards high. The project was funded by a grant from the National Endowment for the Arts and by state funding through the Massachusetts Council on the Arts and Humanities.

A carefully developed Request for Proposals was issued by the Council to solicit contractors to write and produce the *Primer*. The response to this proposal request was overwhelming; never in the agency's history had a Request for Proposals elicited such a large proportion of qualified responses. A design review panel recommended the winning team to the Council Board for approval. The criteria for selection was based on evidence of understanding of the issues, ability to transmit that knowledge to the intended audience, evidence that the *Primer* would be well illustrated, well written, and portray excellent graphic design, and the contractors' ability in teaching, organizing workshops, and working with community

TAKING ACTION

◆ Locate pedestrian assets such as entrances, lobbies, large store windows, arcades, landscaping, public art, and street furnishings such as benches, lights, and trash receptacles where the flow of pedestrians is greatest.

◆ Parking requires both practical and visual consideration. Place access to parking near the greatest volume of traffic (although not near a busy intersection where it can obstruct traffic flow), but hide the parking area itself to whatever extent possible—underground, garaged, or behind buildings and not on the street. Where parking lots do exist on the street, plantings or attractive fences make excellent screens to hide and beautify them.

◆ Match size and massing of new buildings as closely as possible to surrounding architecture except in the case of sprawl development.

◆ Adapt historic buildings for re-use wherever possible.

◆ Allow neighboring historic architecture to influence the size, shape, style, materials, and detailing of new buildings, parks, and street furnishings.

◆ Research local history for clues to significant events or fragments of history in the area. Commemorate these in new developments.

◆ Review drawings to see if buildings fit the natural topography. Support the designer in taking advantage of nature instead of fighting it.

◆ Take advantage of views and sun without depriving others by not placing the tallest parts of the building directly against an existing windowed facade.

◆ Use small pavers such as granite cobbles, bricks, or asphalt units to allow rainwater to seep into the ground rather than running into the street. Turf blocks can be used for parking in small towns and semi-rural areas, and planting of all kinds is very helpful. (Turf blocks are hollow concrete pavers that can be filled and planted with grass, making a durable, but not lush, lawn.)

◆ Use local maps to consider links to nearby open spaces and pedestrian routes and networks, or potential networks.

21

A DESIGN PRIMER FOR CITIES AND TOWNS OFFERS SPECIFIC "TAKING ACTION" SECTIONS SUCH AS THIS ONE FOR IMPLEMENTATION BY COMMUNITIES. (REPRINTED WITH PERMISSION FROM THE MASSACHUSETTS CULTURAL COUNCIL.)

groups and public officials. The design team of Anne Mackin, a writer, planner, and landscape designer; Alex Krieger (in association with Chan Krieger Levi, Architects, Inc.), and Clifford Selbert Design, Inc., graphic designers, was selected by the Council.

Public workshops were an important component of this project; they were held across the state to provide public officials with an opportunity to hear about the ideas from the *Primer* firsthand. We wanted to make sure that the *Primer* was much more than a well-written book that would ultimately end up on a shelf. The workshops offered a chance for a town's compelling questions to be answered and a way for public officials to carry out the lessons contained in the *Primer*. As part of the contract with the Council, six workshops were held around the state. Some were cosponsored with other relevant organizations such as the Massachusetts Mayors Association, which held a design workshop as part of their annual meeting.

The reaction from the field to the *Primer* was overwhelming. Within months one Massachusetts town, Northborough, incorporated the *Primer* into its zoning bylaws as a strongly recommended guide for future developers. Town officials across the country requested copies of the *Primer* for their work in land-use planning. Designers wanted copies to give out to educate their clients. Copies were given to the mayor or chief elected official of all Massachusetts cities and towns, of the boards of selectmen, their planning and zoning boards, every public library in the state, local community development corporations, and the state public development and finance agencies. Other copies were sold at a moderate cost and are available through the Boston Society of Architects. Most importantly, the original goals of this project to expedite discussion and decision making about quality community design were met.

Inspiring Mayors to Action

The Mayors Institute on City Design was the impetus for the *Primer* workshops as a successful example of design advocacy and education. Sponsored by the National Endowment for the Arts, the Institute is held several times a year around the country for a small group of invited mayors. The participants spend three intensive days in the retreat learning about design

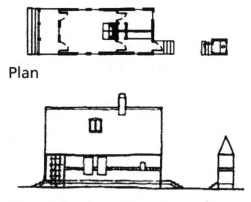

Plan

Elevation

 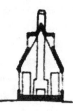

Elevation   Section

   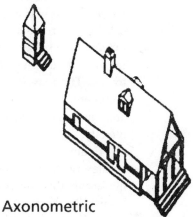

Perspective   Axonometric

THE *DESIGN PRIMER* USES SIMPLE BUT INFORMATIVE ILLUSTRATIONS SUCH AS THESE TO MAKE THE COMPLICATED ISSUES OF ARCHITECTURE UNDERSTANDABLE TO PUBLIC OFFICIALS AND CITIZENS. (REPRINTED WITH PERMISSION FROM THE MASSACHUSETTS CULTURAL COUNCIL.)

and development, grappling with complex and controversial issues without the glare of publicity, and beginning to explore solutions. Mayors return home with a new understanding of the impact of design on their cities. They rethink solutions to old problems and shake up action in their hometowns. If you would like your mayor to benefit from this workshop, contact the Mayors Institute on City Design in Washington, D.C.

The approach to advocacy and learning used by the Mayors Institute on City Design is very strategic. Mayors come to the Institute with a pressing design or development problem for discussion and debate. Each mayor offers a brief presentation describing the controversy or problem. A small core of national experts in design, planning, development, zoning, historic preservation, traffic, engineering, or other relevant issues is invited as a resource team. The resource faculty and other mayors provide suggestions, another point of view, and serve as a further stimulus for debate and learning.

The Mayors Institute on City Design reinforces the role of mayors as the chief designers of cities. The goal of the Institute is not to devise solutions to complex design questions, but rather to offer an *approach* to identifying the problem and a path for solutions. Often a mayor will present a case, only to hear from the resource experts and other mayors that he or she should really be considering another question entirely. One example is a New Hampshire mayor who requested advice on location of a regional shopping mall in his community. Other mayors then spoke from painful experience, describing similar malls that devastated the commercial center of their small towns. The mayor was advised to provide incentives for the commercial redevelopment of the project in the downtown area instead of courting a more remote location on the edge of the city.

Examples of case studies presented at previous Mayors Institutes on City Design reflect the diversity of development questions that mayors must answer. Mayor Abramson of Louisville, Kentucky, wanted strategies to improve a downtown shopping district that contained a convention center, a covered retail center, and a vacant landmark hotel. Mayor Smith of Las Cruces, New Mexico, wanted to reconnect the downtown to nearby neighborhoods and to increase business investment in the vacant buildings along the main street. Mayor Cole of Pasadena, California, explored the impact that transit

THE MAYORS INSTITUTE ON CITY DESIGN GAVE THE MAYOR OF GREEN BAY, WISCONSIN, INVALUABLE ADVICE ON REVITALIZING THE HISTORIC DOWNTOWN AND ADJACENT WATERFRONT. (FROM THE 1993 MAYORS INSTITUTE ON CITY DESIGN, MIDWEST, WASHINGTON UNIVERSITY SCHOOL OF ARCHITECTURE, URBAN RESEARCH AND DESIGN CENTER: JOHN HOAL, DIRECTOR; ROD HENMI, ARTIST.)

development adjacent to an historic depot would have on the downtown and nearby residential neighborhoods. Green Bay, Wisconsin, is divided by the Fox River. Mayor Halloin sought waterfront improvements to draw people to the river while at the same time providing a link to the two sides of the city. Advice received at the Mayors Institute on City Design encouraged him to reconsider the importance of the historic city center and make stronger connections to the waterfront.

Mayors typically return home with new approaches to difficult problems. They have changed their old ways of viewing their cities, reorganized their offices and their approaches to planning and design, become advocates for new ways of development, and better understood the struggles of their own staff and community boards. The U.S. Conference of Mayors sponsors follow-up meetings with alumnae of the Mayors Institute on City Design to continue this advocacy and education. The impact of the Institute on mayors is reflected in the following comment:

The Institute crystallized my thoughts on the importance of down-
towns, and the necessity of pedestrian-friendly, safe, and well-lit
streets and sidewalks without blank walls. I also came home con-
vinced that cities have to take a total design approach to their
downtowns, not just looking at landscaping or streets or parking,
but everything—the mix of uses, the public and private spaces, the
sidewalks, streetlights—everything working together to create a
place where people want to be.

MAYOR BILL HARRIS, LINCOLN, NEBRASKA

The best results occur when mayors return home and take
action. Several mayors offer tangible and often dramatic improvements. After presenting his case on waterfront development of Lake Champlain, Mayor Clavelle of Burlington, Vermont, convinced the city to purchase an eleven-acre tract of
railroad land and turn it into a public park. Two years later, citizens approved $3 million to purchase adjacent parcels for a
shoreline of publicly owned parks and related waterfront activity. Mayor Vialle of Tacoma, Washington, struggled with
ways to connect the city's downtown to its waterfront, due to a
freeway separating the two areas. The Institute gave her the
idea to build a park on the "air-rights" over the freeway as a
way to revitalize the city. Design and engineering plans are now
completed for this project, and funding requests are in place.

Several mayors return from the Institute and sponsor their
own design advocacy forums at home. Mayor Weiner sponsored her own workshop in Savannah, Georgia, for example,
asking citizens to define their vision for the city's future. National experts in design, planning, and development spoke
about the basics of good city design. Mayor Weiner also sought
opinions from downtown residents, merchants, and preserva-
tionists. Mayor Granger of Fort Worth, Texas, took direct
action when she returned from the Institute. She was presented
with designs for an addition to the city library which she considered unacceptable. She invited Mayor Riley of Charleston,
South Carolina, one of the founders of the Mayors Institute, to
talk to city leaders about demanding good urban design. She
then canceled the contract for the library addition and held a
design competition for the library "to get the results she thinks
the city deserves."[14]

The model of the Mayors Institute can be adapted on a local
level to work with discrete city departments in conjunction

with citizen boards, neighborhoods, and businesses. The intensive workshop approach with select projects, individuals, and decision makers could result in productive action on a local, statewide, or regional level.

Vermont Design Institute

The success of the Mayors Institute on City Design was an impetus for the Vermont Council on the Arts to create a mechanism to educate their own local leaders. The Arts Council sponsored a statewide conference on design at the State House in Vermont. This public event was followed by targeted workshops for public leaders and planning officials, modeled after the format of the intensive design retreat atmosphere of the Mayors Institute.

More recently, the Vermont Design Institute was expanded to include hands-on training in design for citizens involved in their communities through volunteer service on planning boards, environmental commissions, local government, and other forums. Although Vermont has a long tradition of community involvement in local decision making, volunteers may have little formal training in the complex issues of design or development. The Vermont Design Institute gives participants a chance to meet in small groups with leading designers, learning from case studies, discussions, and other citizens involved in community decisions about their public environment. Many of the participants serve on planning and conservation commissions and other related boards. Their insight and decision making ability are expanded after this experience.

As you read about the *Primer* workshops, the Vermont Design Institute, or the Mayors Institute on Design, consider sponsoring your own targeted design workshop. What would happen if you could convince a major player in town to convene a forum with five bank presidents? What about including the owners of ten major businesses in your downtown or neighborhood? Target the directors of the public works, community development, planning, and zoning departments, and see what evolves. Work to educate your city council or board of aldermen. The editors of the major newspapers and owners of the radio stations in town pose enormous opportunities, both to be informed and to educate others. The list is endless and limited only by the imagination and energy of you and your coconspirators.

Educating Our Next Generation

The strategies for design advocacy described so far in this book are based on a need for education and technical assistance for the design decision makers, participants, or recipients of the process. Education of *future* decision makers and participants should not be overlooked. Tremendous effort and resources are spent in the education of our children, but most school curricula do not give children an adequate opportunity to learn about design and their community. Furthermore, many schools do not recognize the educational value of design in teaching more traditional classroom material.

Successful design education programs are taking place around the country, but many people are not aware of them. In order to help educators tap into this enormous resource, the Council produced a *Guidebook to Selected Projects in Design Education*. The purpose of this effort was to document and summarize key efforts across the country in design education for schoolchildren and to provide an introduction to implementation of such models elsewhere. The underlying impetus for this project was the firm belief that the children of today are the design decision makers and consumers of tomorrow. With a little luck and some sound planning, education of children can often serve to educate their parents as well.

At the time of our foray into design education, we were surprised at how little information was readily available for parents or educators. As we learned more about this field, we were impressed at the extent that education in design can help schoolchildren integrate learning in social studies, history, mathematics, science, sociology, art, and creative thinking. The basic premise behind design education was described on the first page of the *Guidebook*:

Design education introduces a collaborative process in the classroom complete with the stimulation of critical thinking skills; problem-solving activities; and decision-making skills. Activities often center around planning, creating, inventing, making, doing, reflecting, and generating new ideas. Students may gain practical skills in understanding two- and three-dimensional form through perspective drawing and model-building, and they may learn less tangible skills such as the appreciation and understanding of how a building is built and how a community evolves and is planned.[15]

The *Guidebook* summarized over a hundred project ideas with information on how to organize such projects. Included is an extensive resource list highlighting over 150 organizations, foundations, and clearinghouses that offer programming advice, teaching services, curriculum kits, publications, or funding. The *Guidebook* was distributed free to all the school systems in the state (specifically targeting the superintendents, the curriculum coordinators, and social studies teachers) and to every municipal library and the universities in the state. In addition, copies are available at cost through the Boston Society of Architects.

The development of this publication benefited tremendously from an Advisory Board of educators and designers. They provided vital input to the evolution of this project; they also emphasized how rare it was for a group such as theirs to be formed. Significant collaborations and partnerships continued as a result of this project. (An innovative educational exhibition at the Children's Museum of Boston, based on the transportation and land-use impact of the depression of the Central Artery, the major roadway going through the city, stemmed from information discussed among Advisory Board members.)

Getting educators' attention on design is difficult due to excessive and competing demands on their time. For this reason, we asked the commissioner of the Massachusetts Department of Education to distribute the guidebooks with a cover letter from him emphasizing the importance of this topic and suggesting means of implementation. Having the commissioner's involvement was an important signal to educators throughout the state that this project should be taken seriously and that it had a wide application beyond the arts.

Lessons from design education

A summary of lessons learned from design education includes the following:

- Target existing civic projects for "hands-on" learning for your students
- Identify resources and talent in your school and community
- Decide on the appropriate curriculum and goals for learning
- Adapt successful models for your needs, where possible
- Look for collaborators or practitioners to help teach and inspire

- Leave children with a thirst for learning and the knowledge that they can make a difference in their community

The following examples are drawn from the *Guidebook to Selected Projects in Design Education* and highlight interesting models. In some cases, teachers develop and implement programs that are part of the everyday classroom experience. In the Lawrence High School, for example, students participated in walking tours of the city, particularly the central business district and the industrial mill area. Students researched the site and then prepared drawings of the buildings. Their work resulted in a booklet, *Walking Tour of Lawrence, MA: Canal and Dam Area*, which was used in classes and created an appreciation of the architectural history of the city.

Another approach is to rely on a professional designer or design educator to teach specific information as a complement to the existing curriculum. The Worcester Heritage Preservation Society, for example, meets regularly with students to lead neighborhood discovery tours and to give slide presentations in the classroom to teach about the city's architectural history. Architectural curriculum kits are then loaned to the teacher to introduce architectural concepts to the students.

Often teachers and designers collaborate to develop and implement new curricula. The Historic Neighborhoods Foundation in Boston helps students learn architecture, geography, and the social history of their school and neighborhoods. Architectural treasure hunts and student projects in art and social studies classes are just a few of the techniques applied.

Asking children to visualize the future can provoke imaginative responses. The Boston Society of Architects asked students from schools in five cities to draw their image of their community in the future. Known as "Kids Vision," the project resulted in a traveling art exhibit and extensive coverage on television and in the newspapers. This experiment was held in conjunction with a national "ideas" competition sponsored by the Boston Society of Architects which was seeking future visions for the city.

A tangible example of learning about design and construction was offered through the collaboration of the development company Spaulding and Slye, the Prospect Company, and the New England Telephone Company. Children from the McKay School in East Boston received lessons in art, architecture, engineering, demolition, urban planning, and marketing as applied to construction of a building at 125 High Street in Boston.

"Teach the Teachers" about design and multiply the opportunity to educate children about design and their built environment. This approach is one of several successful models created by the Center for Understanding the Built Environment (CUBE), based in Prairie Village, Kansas, near Kansas City.

THE CENTER FOR UNDERSTANDING THE BUILT ENVIRONMENT GIVES STUDENTS AND TEACHERS HANDS-ON EDUCATION TO BECOME CITY BUILDERS. (COURTESY OF THE CENTER FOR UNDERSTANDING THE BUILT ENVIRONMENT; PHOTOGRAPH BY SKIP BROWN.)

CUBE offers numerous workshops to teach educators about design. According to Ginny Graves, director of CUBE, the most effective way of training teachers is to work with them for several days and then invite them back to share ideas and projects about a month after the workshop is completed.

One of CUBE's most popular activities is "Box City," now in its twenty-fifth year. This program lets children convert cardboard boxes into their own cities while they take on the roles of developers, neighborhood activists, government officials, environmentalists, planners, and designers. With an adaptable curriculum, Box City brings participants into the process, controversies, and difficult decisions faced in development. Related hands-on curriculum materials, such as the "Walk Around the Block" notebook, let students develop a personalized journal of their neighborhood while learning about architecture, city planning, history, economics, politics, geography, science, and art.

Another successful model of bringing architecture education into the public schools was developed by the Foundation for Architecture, a nonprofit organization initially created by the Philadelphia Chapter of the American Institute of Architects. Over 5,000 students are served each year as a result of a strong partnership with volunteers from local architectural firms and architecture students at Temple University and the University of Pennsylvania who lead design activities for schoolchildren. Local school systems contract with the Foundation for Architecture for twenty-five eight-week classroom programs each semester.

Programs are designed to meet the individual needs of the schools. Examples include studies of cities while learning about their physical, social, and economic development, walking tours with hands-on participatory activities, redesigning parts of their own school building, and work with citizens at a geriatric center where the children and residents learn about architecture, city design, and each other. The Foundation for Architecture also sponsors teacher workshops, a resource center for teachers' use, and a sourcebook for classroom projects, *Architecture In Education: A Resource of Imaginative Ideas and Tested Activities*.

The interdisciplinary benefit of design education is a persuasive argument in advocating with schools. The Architecture and Children Program of the School Zone Institute, a nonprofit educational organization based in Albuquerque, New Mexico,

and Seattle, Washington, uses the built environment as a mechanism to integrate academic and artistic disciplines. While learning about architecture, students gain communication and presentation skills and learn to work in groups and to analyze and solve complex problems.

What does it really mean to say that architectural concepts cut across several disciplines? One intriguing response is an approach to learning described by the School Zone Institute. Take the concept of "balance," for example. In architecture and the visual arts, balance refers to form, color, line, space, and texture. In the physical sciences, balance may mean equilibrium of force and structure. In life sciences, ecological balance or the equilibrium of systems may be studied. Mathematics would uncover the concept of balance relating to scale and weight or symmetry and asymmetry. Movement or physical education might explore the balance of bodies in dance, sport, and choreography, which can also serve as illustrations of architectural or engineering principles. The balance of power would be represented through economic or political forces emphasized in social studies.[16] Curriculum materials include posters that guide teachers and students through problem-solving experiences ranging from playground design to city planning.

These few examples indicate the diversity and range of programs possible. Perhaps the biggest challenge in implementing design education is convincing educators to take time and resources from already overcrowded schedules and underfunded programs. The best approach is to integrate learning through existing social studies, art, math, or history programs and to explore the benefits of design as a discipline that integrates and enhances existing curricula. Most cities are fortunate to have experienced designers, engineers, planners, and/or public officials who can offer real-world examples for learning. In addition, don't hesitate to contact local professional design organizations and retired people who have worked in related fields to share their knowledge and to serve as advisors for student projects.

Duplicating Excellence in Education

The examples cited above all share one quality—excellence in education. How can this excellence be duplicated? What factors are critical for success? To answer these questions, the American Institute of Architects' Environmental Education Committee conducted a national study evaluating programs that served over 2,400 schools, 60,000 students each year, 18,000 teachers, and 4,200 architects, artists, and other resource people. Based on this assessment, the major criteria essential for excellence in architectural education for schoolchildren are summarized as follows:

- Clear purpose for the program
- Good leadership and organization
- Well-defined and often multidisciplinary curriculum
- Systematized method of teaching and learning
- Ongoing evaluation
- A broad base of support[17]

According to this study, programs defined as excellent address a targeted need with a clear understanding of the goals for student achievement and their outcomes. Leadership and dedication of the people and the organizations involved are often cited as the most important program strengths. Curriculum programs draw on an interdisciplinary approach to learning, such as language arts, mathematics, art, science, social studies, and physical education. This type of curriculum development requires a variety of learning activities and settings, particularly those which emphasize interactive, visual, and experiential activities. Successful programs constantly conduct evaluation, assessing the effectiveness of teacher training, the success of curriculum development, the rate of program expansion, and recognition of their efforts. The final factor that is essential for successful programs is a broad base of internal and external support. Involvement of schools, teachers, students, community members, architects, designers, institutions, and other resource people contributes to the quality of the program (providing important models for the students) and increases the impact of learning about design for all the participants.

This book explores numerous avenues for advocating better design in your community. Perhaps it is fitting that this chapter ends with a discussion of programs to educate our children, for they truly are our future. If every child were educated to understand the value of good design and to become a creative and compassionate problem solver, then we would be repaid for our efforts through their choices as adult decision makers for our world.

The concluding chapter will give you practical tips to implement your own goals: how to decide where to start, what to do next, and how to carry through the momentum. The key is to decide the best place to start — and then just begin.

Chapter 9

PRACTICAL TIPS FOR ACTION

Designing the City: A Guide for Advocates and Public Officials has introduced many successful approaches to creating more livable communities. If the original intent of this book was successful, you are now inspired to take action yourself or to serve as a catalyst for others. This chapter highlights some practical tips and strategies to help you get going. Consider these points as a guide for you to begin.

You will need to alter some of these pointers for your own circumstances, but the basic approach should be helpful whatever your ultimate objective. These practical tips for action are valuable lessons, even if your goal is not just related to design. Remember, if your overall project or goal seems overwhelming, just break it down into small, manageable tasks. Give yourself a realistic time line, find the most helpful and insightful allies you can, take a deep breath, and begin.

How to Begin

For many people, figuring out just where to start is the hardest part. You may have a general sense of the overall problem, but you are not sure if you are targeting the right issue. Don't be alarmed; this situation is extremely common. You may not be at a point where you can clearly articulate the right issues. If so, consider this stage one in which you meet with potential partners, experts, concerned citizens, or other allies. Often an ideal way to frame your key concerns or opportunities is to brainstorm with the best people you can find. Talk about what you think needs to change. Get *their* advice on how to describe these issues and what questions you should be asking.

Explore Ideas

Ask the Right Questions

In order to get the best answers, you need to ask the right questions. You can always find people with more experience than you to suggest answers, but they need to be asked. If you encounter conflicting answers, which often happens, then you must use your best judgment and intuition, along with your most trusted advisors, to determine the best course of action.

Targeting the most critical or strategic issue is important. You may be concerned, for example, about the deteriorating condition of your downtown. Should you focus on reuse of certain parcels of land, the effectiveness of the Downtown Merchants' Association, parking and transportation issues, or is the real problem an issue of drugs and vandalism?

The more time you give yourself initially to identify the major issues, the more successful your outcome will be. Your research at this stage will also uncover unexpected sources of collaboration and support. The complexities of your issue can be overwhelming in the beginning. Don't hesitate to ask people repeatedly to define the terms in the alphabet soup of issues and organizations you will encounter. It's amazing how quickly you will pick up this language.

Tap the Best Minds

Your early research should consist of many conversations with some of the best thinkers you can identify that are concerned with your issue. Don't be shy about asking the best people you can for advice, even if you have never met them or you think they would never take the time to talk to you. You will be surprised. People like to be asked for advice, and often the most successful people are the most generous with their time. You may need to make many inquiries before you can get through to them, however, so be persistent.

IF YOU PROMISED TO MAKE THE MEETING LAST
NO LONGER THAN THIRTY MINUTES, THEN *DO* IT.

Be prepared for these meetings. Request information beforehand about the organization or group with whom you are meeting, if possible, so you don't waste their time asking the obvious general questions. Use their time wisely. Explain cogently why you are there, and ask for their frank appraisal and advice. Be prepared to hear a response completely different from your point of view. (They may be right.)

Have a preliminary agenda in mind. Anticipate what you hope to learn from each meeting, and direct the course of the conversation to those points. At the same time, be flexible and *listen carefully*. You may have grossly misperceived the key questions or concerns. It is not unreasonable to inquire, "Am I asking you the right questions? Do you have important concerns about this issue that we are not covering? Or is there another direction that would help us meet our goals more effectively?"

SEND FOLLOW-UP NOTES WITH A
BRIEF SUMMARY OF YOUR PROGRESS.

Take notes and record them carefully. In the beginning it is sometimes difficult to discern what is important information, what is common knowledge, and what is a ground-breaking new idea. After you meet with a few people, you can more easily discriminate among the information you receive. You will be surprised how often you can refer back to old notes and see an important new idea that you had glossed over earlier.

LEAVE THE DOOR OPEN FOR FURTHER
COMMUNICATION AND INVOLVEMENT.

This early stage is a good time to include the professional organizations and other interested parties. Ask them to organize a small meeting of about three to five individuals (on their turf) to meet with you. Raise your questions and concerns and seek their advice in this setting.

Getting Access to Leaders and Partners

Sometimes the people taking the initiative for action do not necessarily have the resources or experience to initiate the work. You may be a citizen concerned about a major highway going through your community, but you have no expertise in the area and no clout. You may work in the city's public works department, but you do not have the ear of the director or the mayor. For any advocacy effort, you need to find appropriate partners, sponsors, or people willing to provide the crucial leadership role.

Your early research is often the best place to find potential leaders and partners. You can find these players in many places: experienced citizen advocates, business leaders, the publisher or editor of your local newspaper, professional design societies, Chambers of Commerce, or the director of your city or state agency. More people than you may realize have a voice in what is developed and built in your community, how land is used, and how priorities are set. The window titled "Who Affects Design?" in Chapter 1 provides a quick reference to the broad scope of participants in the design and development process.

MEET WITH AS MANY CREATIVE, .
INFLUENTIAL PEOPLE AS YOU CAN.
KEEP THEM INFORMED OF YOUR PROGRESS.

Remember that leaders or decision makers will welcome an opportunity to focus on your issue if positioned properly. Citizens have more power than you may realize. As a taxpayer and voter you are paying the salaries of all public officials and determine if elected officials keep or lose their job.

If you are having a hard time getting the ear of busy and influential people, offer to meet them at 8:00 A.M. and take only twenty minutes of their time. Call them at 6:00 P.M. when their secretaries may be out of the office and they answer their own telephones. Ask the most talented, creative, and influential people you can find to help. You'll be surprised how often they agree.

Forging a Plan of Action

Extensive groundwork is necessary to determine if your initial assumptions and approach are sound. Will they be valid in the long term? Are other issues more pressing? Are your assumptions based on solid reality or on the views of a forceful minority? How can you gain support? What is your plan of action to accomplish your goals?

Test Your Idea

Your early research meetings and interviews will provide countless ideas, criticisms, reasons why you can't do it, reasons why you can, and reasons why you must. These sessions also identify future sources of support, information, and expertise.

No doubt you will be introduced to the personalities and controversies you will encounter. Once you've collected all this information, how do you sort it all out? First, based on your research, interviews, and intuition, evaluate the most critical ideas and suggestions. Decide which issues seem most compelling, address your cause most clearly, and are most feasible and most likely to accomplish your goals. Carefully determine which concerns are important but may be tackled more effectively by others.

Target an approach in which you can define tangible goals and clearly define outcomes or objectives you are seeking. Try saying to yourself:

How will I know when my efforts have succeeded?
How can I recognize a successful outcome when I see it?
What is my definition of "success"?

Think about what actions, events, results, or changes of opinion need to occur in order to meet your goals. Establish intermediate goals along the way to gauge whether you are on the right track.

LEARN FROM PRECEDENTS OR SUCCESSFUL
EXAMPLES FROM OTHER STATES OR LOCALITIES.
FEW PROBLEMS ARE NEW. ON THE OTHER HAND,
DON'T BE AFRAID TO BREAK NEW GROUND.

Sometimes talking to people with similar experiences in a different profession can be helpful. Advocates in fields such as public health, development, science, the environment, retailing, or historic preservation, for example, face similar challenges. They all must set priorities and goals, obtain citizen or consumer support, get funds and needed resources, identify expertise and talent, secure public approvals, work with bureaucracies, and manage change. The solution for a technological or environmental crisis may not be appropriate for an issue related to historic preservation or cultural facility development, but the process used to reach consensus and support may provide new ideas. Successes and failures from other arenas offer invaluable insights.

Setting Priorities and Goals

The most important part of the plan of action is setting priorities and establishing goals to meet your needs. The more tangible and concrete your goals, the more likely you are to reach them and see success. All goals cannot be easily defined, but work hard until you can state them as clearly as possible. Decide which issue should be tackled first, and consider carefully what you need to accomplish at each stage. Suggested criteria for setting your goals and priorities may include the following:

• Critical need
• Potential for progress to be made
• Initiative does not duplicate efforts of others
• Wise use of resources and talents
• Identifiable constituency who cares about goals and can affect them (or be affected by them)
• Commitment to program/goals by key participants
• Plan of action can accomplish designated goals
• Effort can be achieved within reasonable time frame and cost (*or*, participants are willing to work within a framework of undetermined time frame and cost)
• Impact of project outcome

Selecting the Best Model for Your Needs

Once your goals and priorities are established, set a realistic timetable, budget, and work plan. Start small and build up with incremental successes. Think about the type of action you want to pursue and consider a variety of models. Many successful approaches are suggested throughout this book, and each situation is unique.

Is it best to organize a conference or workshop to stimulate discussion and action? Should you start a small pilot project to target key opportunities? What about creating a public educational campaign? Perhaps for your goals it is wiser to target only the most important decision makers. Do you want to start with small private meetings or a splashy big public event? Is the main need simply a clearinghouse of information? You may find it advantageous to create a visible partnership with relevant organizations or agencies.

Make the Decision

As you make these decisions, consider whether it is better for you to make your efforts political or nonpartisan. Are your collaborators from the public sector, private sector, or a combination? Will you be more effective if you are consciously controversial or carefully neutral? Is your scale of operations local, statewide, regional, national, or international? What are your realistic expectations based on your budget and base of support?

After you develop a model for action, get feedback from some of the same experts you contacted in your first round of investigations. Summarize your preliminary plan of action, your goals and objectives, and a tentative plan of action in a few pages. Share this briefing with many of the people you met earlier. Get their reactions. Revise. Improve. Adjust. Keep an open mind.

Depending on your scale of effort, organization, and goals, develop a more formalized plan of action. It is best to start modestly and succeed, thus strengthening your credibility, rather than trying to tackle too much and thus failing. You may not always have this choice, however, depending on your issue. Beware of that fine line between being too cautious and not allowing yourself to take educated risks.

Finding People Power

Tap the major players, potential partners, citizen groups, professional organizations, and other allies to provide necessary staff and resources. Pick the best talent you can find. Establish an experienced advisory board with a specific function and a short tenure to move your effort forward.

Where can you find staff? Your easiest route, of course, is to convince your own organization of the importance of this task and to allocate staff (perhaps temporarily) for your issue. If you are not associated with an organization, or if this allocation is not possible, seek experienced help in the following locations.

A temporary loan of staff from related agencies or organizations can offer an invaluable burst of experience. You are more likely to be successful with this approach if you have good access to the leadership. Be sure to describe clearly the benefits to the agency if staff is allocated temporarily for your cause. Convincing arguments to use may be the relevance of your mission to the agency's operations, training of staff, economies of operations, and the impact of your project.

Grants from foundations or local, state, or federal government can be an essential, though often temporary, source of funds for staff, consultants, and other needed resources. The time lag from application to receipt of funds can seem interminable (and often is), but the very process of applying for grants and obtaining letters of support can clarify your own goals and work plan and can strengthen the commitment of others working with you. Even if the funding request is not accepted, you will have a process defined, support mustered, and be in a much better position to obtain your funding elsewhere.

Business volunteers offer a wide range of talent and resources. Do not overlook the commitment of corporations in your community to provide short-term expertise, and don't be afraid to ask. Be as explicit as you can in your needs. Try to define how this work will benefit the company, such as providing a public service to the community and good will to the company, improving the quality of your town and therefore encouraging skilled workers to locate there, providing training in different skills to the volunteers, and offering important contacts for the business.

Retired people are often underutilized. Their experience, point of view, commitment to their community, expertise, and time availability are important assets. Contact the Small Business Administration, a federal agency with offices in every state, which runs the "SCORE" program for coordinating the services of retired senior citizens with business expertise. You may also identify volunteers through the Retired Senior Volunteer Program, known as RSVP. Many localities have other mechanisms to identify volunteer opportunities.

Citizen volunteers offer unparalleled dedication and commitment. Logical places to identify volunteers include neighborhood associations, downtown business groups, Chambers of Commerce, League of Women Voters, Parent-Teacher Associations, civic associations, professional organizations, or garden clubs. In one town, for example, the local Boy Scouts hand-delivered a final report detailing rural design proposals to every house in their community. This task benefited the town, introduced the boys to rural design issues, and ensured that the reports were distributed effectively.

Colleges and universities provide essential support and expertise. Faculty often seek real-life examples for teaching, and students need work experience for learning. The most successful outcomes occur when you define the tasks extremely clearly, agree in the beginning on mutual expectations for the final products, and narrow your focus. Most student projects suffer from trying to accomplish too much. You can get the most from students if you have an energetic and knowledgeable faculty supervisor. An ideal situation is to convince the faculty member to devote a workshop to your topic. Faculty involvement and adequate supervision are essential. To obtain student and faculty support, contact the dean or chairman of the department most relevant to your issue at a college or university and request referral to an appropriate faculty member.

As you plan your staffing needs, consider a short-term consulting arrangement to get the tasks in motion. The level and type of expertise you need will change over time. Shorter term consultations provide expertise and a high energy level for a specific need. This arrangement is often useful to supplement skills of your existing staff or to provide another point of view.

CREATE AN ADVISORY BOARD OF THE BEST
TALENT YOU CAN FIND. PROMISE THEM A TOTAL
OF ONLY THREE TO FIVE SHORT MEETINGS.

As your project evolves, consider an Advisory Board to give you unparalleled experience and a supportive forum for exploring ideas. Select a diverse group of people with an interest in your cause who represent the absolute top of their field. Aim for the best people you can find and use their time judiciously. Be clear on what you hope to accomplish with this group, and keep the meetings short and focused. Keep them involved and give them credit.

THE ADVISORY BOARD PROVIDES AN
IMPORTANT BALANCE, SOUNDING BOARD,
AND OPPORTUNITY TO MEET WITH THE BEST
MINDS YOU CAN COLLECT, WHILE ADDING
LEGITIMACY TO YOUR EFFORT.

Remember that people are often looking for a meaningful way to offer their services, but they do not know where they are needed, they do not realize what they do every day in their job is considered a valuable skill by others, or they just don't take the initiative to volunteer. Be sure their time is used well, focused, and that they are acknowledged appropriately for their efforts. People must also see where their actions made a difference to your overall effort.

The Eternal Search for Funding

The most important resource in accomplishing your goals is people, not money. Many of the suggestions for staffing listed above can be secured without a long-term commitment of dollars. Nevertheless, you can not ignore the fact that you need access to resources to communicate with others, get your message heard, and put your plan into action. Where should you begin?

Once you have identified your issues clearly and organized your initial team of supporters, you need funding for a base of operation. It can be as simple as a post office box or home address and telephone. As you muster your forces you will benefit from collaborators to help you proceed. Nonprofit organizations or professional associations may find it in their interest (and yours) to join forces with you, offering you a place of operation and expanding both your legitimacy and theirs. Think creatively to determine who would find it in their interest to work with you.

Getting public funds

Local, state, and federal agencies all offer grant programs for projects that benefit communities. The difficulty is figuring out which agency has a program to serve your needs, comprehending the maze of regulations, and then writing a competitive grant application. Guidelines, priorities for funding, staff, and leadership change frequently.

If you feel overwhelmed by the extensive listing of government agencies in the back of your local telephone book, ask for help. It can be frustrating to try to comprehend the alphabet soup of government agencies, but when funds are available, these agencies can make a difference in your ability to operate. Don't hesitate to call the Public Information Department at your city hall or contact your legislative leadership to help you through this maze. Most offices have a small staff who can help you identify possible sources of funding. Be persistent. Your taxes are paying their salaries.

Spending fifteen minutes poring through a directory of federal, state, or local agencies will give you a broader picture of the possibilities. A brief sampling of federal, regional, state, or local sources of public funding might include the following departments: community development, housing, transportation, environmental affairs, public works, arts and humanities, economic and industrial development, and numerous independent boards and commissions.

Foundations and the private sector

In contrast to the lengthy process of most public funding, support from the private sector and foundations can happen much more quickly. The key here is your ability to frame your request in a manner to match the foundations' priorities. Foundations and corporations typically have established guidelines and procedures for giving grants. Others may be willing to provide specific grants for a unique issue that relates to a personal or business interest of the leaders in the company.

Some foundations are more receptive to applications from organizations with which they have an association. Do not be

TIPS FOR WRITING A SUCCESSFUL PROPOSAL

1. Be sure your grant request meets the criteria of the sponsoring organization. *Read* every word of the guidelines and application form carefully, and follow all their requirements to the absolute letter.

2. Be clear and concise in your written proposal. Do not use jargon. Make sure someone who is not intimately involved with your cause reads and can understand your proposal before you submit it.

3. Present a clear case. Carefully outline your need, your objectives, how you plan to meet your goals, your work plan, and your budget. Present a convincing case as to why your proposal meets the needs or interest of the funding source.

4. Provide a range of letters of support, demonstrating the importance and impact of your proposal.

5. Keep in contact with the sponsoring organization. If they fund your proposal, give them proper credit. Keep them informed, and come back for the next stage of funding. Often organizations, foundations, and individuals like to continue to support projects they have funded previously.

6. If your proposal is rejected, find out why. You might be able to adapt your request to meet their requirements in the next round. The grant review panel may have valuable criticism to help you better focus your proposal for your next request. Funding organizations tend to know each other, and if they cannot meet your needs, they may suggest someone else who can.

7. Don't give up. Keep trying. And good luck!

shy in asking all your acquaintances to tap their well-connected friends for possible leads. Examine the board composition of foundations or major corporations in your area. You can research foundations and corporations through directories in your local library.

Look carefully at significant businesses in your community for support. Major corporations, contractors, design or engineering firms, professional associations, unions, building construction suppliers, landscaping contractors, or others may provide funding, services, or technical assistance. For most initial inquiries, a well-written, convincing letter that clearly outlines the purpose and expected results from your request, followed up by a well-placed phone call, is the place to begin. If your request for dollars can not be met, ask for other assistance, such as in-kind services, materials, personnel support, substantive ideas, or suggestions of other sources of funds.

Once you identify the right source of funds, you will need to write a proposal. Proven tips for writing a successful proposal are presented in the accompanying window. Some of the ideas will seem self-evident, but you would be surprised how many people do not follow these basic principles.

Building and Maintaining a Constituency

Public participation should be an important part of your advocacy. Decide who will be affected by your project, who you hope to benefit, and who you might harm. Adapting to any change is difficult for many people. Consider seriously how the public will be involved in your decision making and action and how "the public" is defined in your case. Keep communication open within the various groups with whom you are working, both formally and informally.

Do not confuse public participation with telling other people what you are doing. Give them a chance to respond to your views and goals. Remember that listening is much more than nodding in the right places. Your project will be stronger if you can respond to the different concerns within the community. It is much better to confront conflict in a managed way up front than to have people complain about your effort privately (or worse yet publicly) and then shoot you down.

You can build your constituency through different avenues. Obvious sources of support are people and organizations who are sympathetic to your point of view or affected directly by the issue in question. Possible constituencies or collaborators could include the abutters, other neighbors, statewide interest groups, other states with similar concerns, regional or national organizations, schools and educational institutions, professional associations, other advocacy organizations, cultural institutions, the clergy, legislative leadership, and the media.

Partners can be found in unexpected places. The Bricklayers Union in Boston sponsored award-winning affordable housing. State arts agencies and public works agencies work together on design. McDonald's sponsored a national design competition. Churches and synagogues work together to build affordable housing. Cities build gardens next to wastewater treatment plants and public art sculpture gardens at electric generating stations. The opportunities are endless.

Keep people informed

The key to building and maintaining a constituency is to keep people informed and educated. Include your collaborators and your constituents in your process. Give them a role whenever possible. Be responsive to their needs and concerns, and learn what you can from their point of view. Identify their talent and expertise and use it to further your cause. Share any credit with your partners and collaborators. You will strengthen the credibility of your group and bring in important allies.

The need for public education must be reinforced continually. Education and awareness are the most potent tools of any advocate. Start a newsletter, write convincing articles in newsletters, sponsor conferences and symposia, distribute pamphlets, use the press, invite dialog, debate, even create controversy when it will further your cause.

The media as an ally

Consider the media an important ally. Use newspapers, magazines, radio, and television to spread your message. Identify reporters and writers interested in your issue and keep them informed behind the scenes. They will be much more receptive to your story when the big moment comes. A well-placed news item can help more than you realize in making your cause known.

Translate your issue to understandable language. Learn what makes a news story. Emphasize people, not process and plans. How will people's lives be affected if you are successful—or if you are not? Controversy, crises, results, and human interest stories make the news.

Make it easy for the media to understand your mission and to follow up with their own stories. You cannot control what the media ultimately produces, but you can make your story heard by providing them with a compelling but succinct statement of your purpose, its significance, relevant factual information, and ready access to stories. When preparing press releases don't forget the "who, what, when, where, and why" in the first paragraph. Highlight newsworthy aspects that can be translated into short segments for television and radio broadcast. For the print media write a newsworthy one-page press release. Include quotable comments by key figures. Offer a black and white photograph, if possible, and name a contact for more information. Follow up with a phone call to the news source, be persistent and keep the momentum going.

Legislative action

Do not underestimate the power of legislative action and advocacy. Involve your local, state, and national legislative leaders. Most of these public officials have their own press offices that will help you if you acknowledge the legislators. Work together on the media strategy. State and local public agencies also have press and public information offices that may provide assistance.

Use your constituents to influence legislative action. Keep abreast of proposed legislation that affects your project. Better yet, work with your public officials to propose your own legislation for the public good. When you learn that an issue is to be voted on by a legislative body, muster your forces. Set up legislative briefing sessions and a phone chain. Most likely you will work with the legislator's staff, not the legislator, but your message will still be heard. Just a few phone calls in support of a bill often determines the outcome of the legislator's vote.

Building and maintaining a constituency is an iterative and ongoing process. Citizen participation, public forums, pilot projects, and public awareness and understanding are all essential. Working with the media and your legislators reinforces your efforts. Create projects that capture the imagination and support of your constituents to make a difference.

Find what works best for you

What kind of programs or incentives work best? What models or pilot projects serve as catalysts to convince others of the validity of your point of view? How can you lead by example? How can you influence change for the long term? How can you make a difference? The answers, of course, depend on the goals you establish for your own endeavor and the resources, energy, and talent you are able to coalesce. Use the strategies for effective action presented in this book to make a difference in your community, and then share your successes with others.

DESIGN ARTS PROGRAMS IN OTHER STATES

Several states have created Design Arts Programs that offer a variety of grant programs, individual fellowships, and other specific initiatives. Current programs are summarized below; their models may provide ideas for action on other state or local levels. For further information on specific programs, contact the state arts council directly.[18]

Alabama State Council on the Arts and Humanities
Design Alabama, Inc.

> One Dexter Avenue
> Montgomery, Alabama 36130
> (205) 261-4076

Design Alabama, Inc. is a separate nonprofit organization established by the state arts council to create awareness and appreciation of the design disciplines. Design Alabama publishes a journal entitled *Design Alabama: The Public Forum for Design in Alabama* and produced a video entitled *Designing*

Alabama: Planning and Design for Community Growth. In addition, their Community Design Assistance Program provides professional design assistance to towns across the state.

Arizona Commission on the Arts

417 West Roosevelt Street
Phoenix, Arizona 85003
(602) 255-5882

The design-related programming at the Commission emphasizes cultural facilities planning and development as well as graphic design. The Design Program is now integrated with the Public Art Program. The Commission supported the publication *Public Art Works: The Arizona Models,* which evaluated public art planning. Their grant program, "Arizona: The Look of Communities," provides funds for consultants for design projects for Arizona's communities, such as streetscape plans for public art, street furniture and signage for historic or arts districts, and historic preservation plans. A related Design Program provides funding to arts organizations, municipalities, and other nonprofit organizations for design-related projects such as conferences, workshops, and design exhibitions.

Arts Midwest

528 Hennepin Avenue
Suite 310
Minneapolis, Minnesota 55403
(612) 341-0755

This regional arts agency conducted a survey and needs assessment on design arts activities in their nine member states as a first step to establishing a regional design arts program for the midwest. This work was followed by a regional retreat on design to further define models and opportunities for design arts programming by Arts Midwest, state arts agencies, and other possible partners. The workshop served to strengthen regional networks among leading design professionals, cultural activists, and government agencies, identified critical needs related to design arts, and targeted next steps for action.

D.C. Commission on the Arts and Humanities

410 8th Street, N.W.
Washington, D.C. 20004
(202) 724-5613

The D.C. Commission on the Arts and Humanities established a Design Arts Grant Program that funded local arts and community groups in design-related projects. The Commission also sponsored a day-long conference on neighborhood design in conjunction with local professional design organizations, other city agencies, state arts councils, and the general public to generate ideas and share information about community design.

Florida Department of State—Division of Cultural Affairs
The Capital
Tallahassee, Florida 32399-0250
(904) 487-2980

The newly created Design Arts Program began with the Florida Design Arts Awards which recognized collaboration among design disciplines in private and public facilities. An Art in State Buildings Program, in effect since 1979, provides for the acquisition or commissioning of art for new state buildings.

Illinois Arts Council
State of Illinois Center
100 West Randolph, Suite 10-500
Chicago, Illinois 60601
(312) 814-6750

The Building by Design Program emphasized the role of the arts as an equal partner with community economic development. The program was established to integrate the planning and design of cultural facilities into the community planning process. Cultural facility development is supported throughout the state through workshops and grants for planning, needs assessment, market feasibility, and design.

Iowa Arts Council
Department of Cultural Affairs
Capitol Complex
Des Moines, Iowa 50319
(515) 281-4451

The Iowa Town Squares program is a collaborative effort between the Iowa Arts Council and Iowa State University's College of Design. The program was created to reaffirm the purpose and value of town squares in the cultural and economic life of the community. Grants sponsor multidiscipline design team residencies in the community.

Kansas Arts Commission
Jayhawk Tower, Suite 1004
700 Jackson
Topeka, Kansas 66603-3714
(913) 296-3335

Design Arts Planning Grants are offered to encourage cooperation among design professionals, local governmental officials, arts organizations, and the public in planning and implementing plans for creation of arts facilities. Several of the grants have supported city-wide cultural planning activities. A roster of Design Arts consultants are paid by the Kansas Arts Commission and community organizations for design-related activities. Some of this work has resulted in a Capital Aid Grant for arts activities, which is funded by the Commission. A periodic newsletter, "Design Arts Matters," is also published.

Louisiana Division of the Arts
P.O. Box 44247
Baton Rouge, Louisiana 70804
(504) 342-8180

The Project Assistance Program provides matching grant support for community-supported arts projects that promote excellence in the design fields. Design activities such as feasibility studies, schematic projects, competitions, collaborations, theory and research, projects that demonstrate the benefits of design excellence, and projects that educate the public about design are eligible for funding.

Maine Arts Commission
Station 25
Augusta, Maine 04333
(207) 289-2724

The Three Cities Project evaluated urban development and design review in three of Maine's cities: Bangor, Lewiston, and Portland. Most recently, in conjunction with the University of Southern Maine and the State Department of Economic and Community Development's Bureau of Comprehensive Planning, a "visual assessment manual" entitled *The Hidden Design of Land Use Ordinances* was prepared. It is particularly useful for towns involved in the state-mandated comprehensive land-use planning.

Massachusetts Cultural Council (formerly Massachusetts Council on the Arts and Humanities)

120 Boylston Street
Boston, Massachusetts 02116
(617) 727-3668

The former Design and Development Program of the Massachusetts Council on the Arts and Humanities included a multi-faceted approach to design advocacy, education, technical assistance, and funding. The Council initiated a number of pilot design projects with other state agencies, including a bridge design project with the Massachusetts Department of Public Works, a highway landscape design project with the Massachusetts Turnpike Authority, and a Community Design Assistance Program for funding of design projects in downtowns in conjunction with the Main Street Program of the Executive Office of Communities and Development. Smaller towns in the state were later aided through the Rural Design Assistance Program in conjunction with the Center for Rural Massachusetts. The Council worked with the Executive Office of Administration and Finance and twelve other state agencies responsible for finance and development to create state agency policies on design. A Governor's Design Awards Program recognized public- and private-sector design projects of excellence. Educating public officials was the goal of the *Primer on Design* and related workshops around the state. Educating children was the goal of the *Guidebook to Selected Projects in Design Education*. Technical assistance and funding supported the development of artists housing and cultural facilities in the Cultural Facilities Technical Assistance Program and the Space Program. A video, *Creating Artists Space*, served as an important advocacy tool. A new partnership, called the Massachusetts Facilities Fund, between the Massachusetts Cultural Council, the New England Foundation for the Arts, and the New York–based Cultural Facilities Fund provides funds for technical assistance, below-market loans, and loan guarantees for cultural facility development. The approach used to create all of these programs and the lessons learned are described in more detail throughout this book.

New England Foundation for the Arts

678 Massachusetts Avenue
Cambridge, Massachusetts 02139
(617) 492-2914

The most current design- and community-related project of this regional consortium of state arts agencies was a regional conference entitled *Broadening Our Vision: Connecting the Arts and Community Development.* The goal of this initiative was to create partnerships between leaders in the arts, community development, and foundations. This workshop was cosponsored with the Massachusetts Association of Community Development Corporations and led to commitments for a new grant program to support collaborations between the arts and community development. The New England Foundation for the Arts previously offered mini-grants to their member organizations to support design arts projects. In addition, the Foundation developed two directories of cultural facilities in the New England states on performing arts and visual arts facilities.

New Jersey State Council on the Arts

20 West State Street
State Office Building No. CN 306
Trenton, New Jersey 08625
(609) 292-6130

A state-funded design arts fellowship program was a key component of this example. The Council also conducted workshops on design initiatives for state and local officials and professional design societies as well as a state design arts conference.

New York State Council on the Arts

915 Broadway
New York, New York 10010
(212) 614-2900

The Architecture, Planning, and Design Program's main role is to award grants for the general operations of design-oriented nonprofit organizations in New York State, as well as project grants for public education efforts and design and planning studies. Funds for rehabilitation of cultural facilities are also available. The Council initiates special projects, such as a national design competition for in-fill housing, an exhibit, publications, and workshops on various design-related topics.

North Carolina Arts Council

Department of Cultural Resources
Raleigh, North Carolina 27601-2807
(919) 733-2111

The "Design Initiatives" funding category enables nonprofit organizations to work to improve the livability of North Carolina communities through the Design Arts. Typical projects include exhibitions, lecture series, workshops, conferences, and special programs that increase public understanding about the value of good design. Important lessons learned from these projects are documented in a publication, *Community Design— Six Case Studies of Cultural Revitalization.* In a separate Management and Technical Assistance Program, a team of consultants are available to help with cultural facility planning and development, artists' work spaces, and other design-related community projects. Funds are also available for implementation of selected projects.

The North Carolina Arts Council took the initiative in creating an unusual and successful partnership called "Pride in Place" between the North Carolina Arts Council, the South Carolina Arts Commission, the Tennessee Arts Commission, and the Main Street Programs of the three states. This program provided technical assistance through resource teams and follow-up consultants to help communities link the quality of life and community design issues to economic development and cultural planning.

Ohio Arts Council

727 East Main Street
Columbus, Ohio 43205
(614) 466-2613

The Ohio Arts Council works toward excellence in the Design Arts through grants for project and residency programs to nonprofit organizations in the state. The Council produced a slide/tape and video presentation entitled *Design: The Art of It All,* which demonstrates the ways design affects our daily lives. Residencies and fellowships are offered to professional designers, and technical assistance is offered to arts organizations. The program "Design for Ohio: Design for Excellence" enabled rural and larger communities in the state to work on design projects.

South Carolina Arts Commission

1800 Gervais Street
Columbia, South Carolina 29201
(803) 734-8696

The South Carolina Arts Commission recently completed work with their Statewide Design Arts Planning Task Force to develop long-range planning for their Design Arts Program over the next decade. The Commission plans to work in cooperation with related institutions in the state to provide forums for design excellence, to attract tourists, and to make South Carolina communities more livable.

Southern Arts Federation

181 14th Street, N.E., Suite 400
Atlanta, Georgia 30309-7603
(404) 874-7244

The Southern Arts Federation, a regional arts agency serving nine states, created a Southern Design Arts Task Force to identify regional design arts issues, define the needs of the design community, establish a communication network among design constituents in the South, and determine an appropriate role for the Southern Arts Federation with respect to the design arts. The Task Force defined the mission of the Southern Arts Federation in this capacity to provide leadership and support:

To assist the South in developing livable communities, with a sense of pride of place, a vision for the future, and a plan of action, guided by commitment to design excellence, sustained economic development, and the preservation and enhancement of the South's unique character and history.

The Federation currently is pursuing ways to accomplish this mission, such as possibly producing a Community Design Resource Book, developing a Southern Community Design Network, advocating a Governors' Community Design Council, and launching a public awareness campaign concerning community design and economic prosperity.

State Arts Council of Oklahoma

Room 640
Jim Thorpe Building
Oklahoma City, Oklahoma 73105-4987
(405) 521-2931

The DesignWorks Program grew out of a productive partnership between the State Arts Council and the Main Street Program of the Oklahoma Department of Commerce. The Oklahoma Foundation for Architecture is a new partner assuming a leadership role with this initiative. DesignWorks brings professional design expertise to rural communities to support their development, revitalization, and preservation efforts. A combination of the *Community DesignBook*, design video, and a dedicated team of professional advisors work together to help improve public spaces of downtowns throughout Oklahoma.

Utah Arts Council

617 East Temple Street
Salt Lake City, Utah 84102
(801) 533-5895

The Utah Design Arts Program emphasizes rural community design, culminating in a *Rural Community Revitalization Manual*. The Utah Arts Council established a Design Arts Resource Center as a clearinghouse for design ideas, associations, publications, and services. The Council also holds regional design symposia to introduce the design professions to graduating high school students. Included in the Design Arts Program is implementation of the state's "One Percent for Art" requirement to acquire works of art for new state buildings.

Vermont Council on the Arts, Inc.

133 State Street
Montpelier, Vermont 05602
(802) 828-3291

Three ongoing programs comprise the core of Vermont's Design Arts Program. The Vermont Design Institute is an intensive two-day retreat for volunteer local planners, based on the model of the NEA's Mayors Institute on Design. Community Design Grants are given to help cities and towns with their own design issues, emphasizing public participation in the design process and increasing access to the public realm for people with disabilities. The Vermont Council on the Arts is working jointly with the Vermont Department of Education and the Vermont Alliance for Arts Education to increase design education in the schools. Previously, the Vermont Council on the Arts sponsored the Vermont Timber Bridge Design Competition, which received national recognition. The winning bridge design has been constructed. The Council also developed and distributed widely a publication encouraging preservation of the rural character of land when siting new housing (*Protecting Your Property Investment Through Good Site Design: A Guide to Siting New Houses in Rural Vermont*).

West Virginia Department of Culture and History

Arts and Humanities Division
Capitol Complex
Charleston, West Virginia 25305
(304) 348-0240

Project 20/21 was created to encourage arts organizations and communities to develop long-range plans to advance their work for the 21st century. The Design Program/Images component of Project 20/21 provides support for building design, feasibility studies, graphic image development, exhibition design, and design conferences.

URBAN DESIGN GLOSSARY: KEY DESIGN AND PLANNING TERMS

access—spaces which accommodate people with special needs, e.g. persons with handicaps or the elderly.

accessory use—a use incidental to, and on the same lot as, a principal use, such as a detached garage apartment on a residential lot.

adaptive use—conversion of a building into a use other than that for which it was designed, such as changing a warehouse into a gallery space or housing.

air rights—(see *transfer of development rights*) the ownership or control which allows the use of air space over property such as buildings, highways, and railroad tracks.

amenity—design features which are valued by the users of a building or public space. Examples of amenities include good architecture, open space, landscaping, seating, an outdoor amphitheater, and public art.

architectural drawings—used by architects and other design professionals during the design process. An *axonometric drawing* appears three-dimensional and is generally an overhead view. An *elevation* is an two-dimensional drawing which shows a facade or side of a structure. A *perspective* also creates the illusion of three-dimensionality, but with reference to relative depth or distance. The *plan* illustrates the room layout, as well as the placement of windows and doors. A *section* cuts through the structure, illustrating wall thicknesses and ceiling heights.

axis–a real or imaginary straight line around which the parts of a structure or plan are symmetrically or evenly arranged or composed.

This glossary reprinted with the permission of the National Trust for Historic Preservation and the Mayors Institute on City Design.

165

axonometric—see *architectural drawings*

background buildings—buildings that may lack exemplary character or significance but are essential to creating a sense of place.

barrier—see *edge, hard*

buffer—a strip of land identified on a site plan or by a zoning ordinance, established to protect one type of land use that is incompatible. Normally, the area is landscaped and kept in open space.

building cap—maximum allowable construction in a designated area or city. For example, San Francisco limits annual downtown office space construction to 475,000 square feet and Petaluma, California, limits the number of residential building permits issued annually.

buildout—the maximum allowable buildable area as stipulated by land use controls like zoning or a building cap.

bulk—see *mass*

certified historic structure—for the purposes of the federal preservation tax incentives, any structure subject to depreciation as defined by the Internal Revenue Code that is listed individually in the *National Register of Historic Places* or located in a registered historic district and certified by the Secretary of the Interior as being of historic significance to the district.

certified rehabilitation—any *rehabilitation* of a certified historic structure that the Secretary of the Interior's standards have determined is consistent with the historic character of the property or the district in which the property is located.

charette—a French term for an intensive collaborative design exercise that generates ideas for a project or plan.

circulation—movement patterns of pedestrians and vehicular traffic.

cluster development—a development design technique that concentrates buildings in specific areas on a site to allow the remaining land to be used for recreation, common open space, and preservation of environmentally sensitive areas. Units are grouped on a smaller land parcel for each unit than specified as the minimum lot size for an individual unit, but the average density for the zone must be maintained.

collaboration—a team effort with the contribution of professionals in different fields, such as architects, landscape architects, engineers, and artists.

colonnade—a linked row of columns providing shade and protected passage.

compatibility—**1.** the characteristics of different uses or activities which allow them to be located near each other in harmony. Some elements affecting compatibility include intensity of occupancy as measured by dwelling units per acre; floor area ratio; pedestrian or vehicular traffic.

Also, complementing uses may be compatible, like residential and retail uses. **2.** the characteristics of different designs which allow them to be located near each other in harmony, such as *scale,* height, materials, and *fenestration.*

comprehensive plan—(see *masterplan*) a broad-reaching general plan for a large area such as a state, county, or municipality. Elements of the plan may include land use, housing, natural resources, traffic and circulation, hazard, and even child care.

cornice—the top of a wall or building element made evident by an assembly of projecting moldings which strike a definitive limit to that section of the building.

demolition by neglect—the destruction of a building through abandonment or lack of maintenance.

density—measurement of the number of units, e.g., housing, or persons per acre, which may indicate the level of activity in an area.

design competition—a way to select design professionals not merely on the basis of reputation but on the basis of a specific response to a project at hand. A competition may take a variety of forms, but it should always include a program, which defines the project, and a jury made up of design professionals as well as local representatives.

design guidelines—criteria established to direct development. Good guidelines offer options without restricting, reflect community image and character, and should be determined prior to the *Request for Proposals (RFP).*

design review board—a municipal body, generally made up of designers and laymen and appointed to serve by the city council, which reviews the design component of proposed developments or modifications to existing developments, generally within a specified area.

directional emphasis—refers to the predominant emphasis of the building, either horizontal or vertical. Recognizing this aspect of design is especially important when designing additions to historic buildings or when planning a new development in a historic district.

dismantling—taking apart a structure piece by piece, often with the intention of reconstructing it elsewhere.

displacement—the movement of individuals, businesses, or industries from property or neighborhoods because of economic development activities like redevelopment, *eminent domain,* or *gentrification.*

district—an area which has a distinct character or purpose, such as an area with predominantly historic buildings, arts facilities, ethnic residents, or unique topography.

easement—a less-than-fee interest in real property acquired through donation or purchase and carried as a deed restriction or covenant to protect important open spaces, views, building facades, and interiors.

edges—delineation of districts or areas which could be physical in nature (e.g., medieval walls or greenbelts) or psychological (e.g., major street joining residential and commercial districts). *Hard edges* create a break between areas. Freeways and busy thoroughfares are generally disruptive hard edges, which create a physical or psychological barrier. *Soft edges* create a subtle break or transition between areas or uses and, unlike hard edges, are not particularly difficult to cross. For instance, a plaza, a park, or a nonoffensive change in land use is considered a soft edge.

elevation—see *architectural drawings*

eminent domain—the power of government to acquire private property for public use for which the owner must receive "just compensation." Redevelopment authorities, state universities, and special districts may also be empowered with eminent domain to acquire parcels of land for economic development uses, infrastructure, and other uses deemed in the public interest.

enclosure (sense of)—an experience in which a pedestrian feels sheltered with a semiprivate realm. Trees, narrow streets, awnings and canopies, and articulated edges create a sense of enclosure.

environmental impact—influence of a development on the natural or built environment.

environmental simulation—images graphically representing the impact of proposed changes to the built or natural environment. The technology is generated by a combination of computer, photographic, and film media. In the case of a proposed skyscraper, simulations may forecast the visual impact of the building as seen from several points in the city. Also, the simulation can forecast how the position of the structure will influence street and sidewalk conditions like shadows and wind.

equity—cash investment (as opposed to mortgage debt) in a project. *Sweat equity* is the investment of occupants' own labor in rehabilitation work.

extended use—any process that increases the useful life of an old building, e.g., adaptive use or continued use.

fabric (e.g., urban fabric)—the physical material of a building, structure, or city, connoting an interweaving of component parts.

facade—the exterior wall of a building exposed to public view or that wall viewed by persons not within the building.

facadism—the retention of only the facade of a historic building during conversion while the remainder is severely altered or destroyed to accept a new use.

FAR (floor area ratio)—a formula for determining permitted building volume as a multiple of the area of the lot. The FAR is determined by dividing the gross floor area of all buildings on a lot by the area of the lot.

For example, a 6 FAR on a 5,000-square-foot lot would allow a building with gross area of 30,000 square feet.

fenestration—design elements of the exterior (architectural) window treatments such as pattern, rhythm, and ornamentation.

gentrification—the process by which young professionals or "gentry" buy into inner-city areas as part of a neighborhood preservation trend, informally contributing to inner-city economic development. Gentrification often causes social tensions as real estate sales and increased real estate values price out and displace lower-income families, many of whom were renters.

greenbelt—a complete or partial ring of open space (green) encircling a city, usually at the urban fringe.

grid—a traditional city plan, based on streets and alleys which are (primarily) perpendicular to one another (e.g., map reads like a grid). New York, Chicago, and Los Angeles are examples of grid cities. The grid pattern is often efficient from a traffic engineering standpoint and offers ease in orientation and way-finding.

growth management—the use of a *comprehensive plan* to regulate new development, based on constraints such as infrastructure availability, delivery of services, and environmental protection.

historic district—a geographically definable area with a significant concentration of buildings, structures, sites, spaces, or objects unified by past events, physical development, design, setting, materials, workmanship, sense of cohesiveness, or related historical and aesthetic associations. The significance of a district may be recognized through listing in a local, state, or national landmarks register and may be protected legally through enactment of a local historic district ordinance administered by a historic district board or commission.

historic rehabilitation tax credit—the Tax Reform Act of 1986 permits owners and some lessees of historic buildings to take a 20 percent income tax credit on the cost of rehabilitating such buildings for industrial, commercial, or rental residential purposes. The rehabilitated building must be a *certified historic structure* that is subject to depreciation, and the rehabilitation must be certified as meeting standards established by the National Park Service.

homesteading—programs under which abandoned buildings are made available at little or no cost in return for an agreement to rehabilitate and occupy them for a specified period of time.

imageability—that quality in a physical object which gives it a high probability of evoking a strong image [physical form or shape] in any given observer. It is that shape, color, or arrangement which facilitates the making of vividly identified, powerfully structured, highly useful mental images of the environment.

infill—housing or other development in an urban area that is designed to fill a void left by vacant property, such as redevelopment land. Generally, the purpose of infill is to revitalize the surrounding area.

inventory of cultural resources—(also called *survey*) a list or matrix of cultural resources within a community or area. The inventory is a valuable tool for maximizing the use of existing facilities and assessing needs for new and improved facilities.

landmark—**1.** a structure or feature of historical, cultural, or architectural significance (see *National Historic Landmark*). **2.** an object that is useful for orientation. This term is used without regard to historic value and can describe a parking structure as well as a monument.

landmarks register—a listing of buildings, districts, and objects designated for historical, architectural, and other special significance that may carry protection for listed properties.

leapfrog development—development that occurs well beyond the existing limits of urban development and thus leaves the intervening vacant land behind and results in sprawl.

linkage—tying one sort of development to a related service, i.e., requiring office space developers to provide a certain number of housing units or adjunct services like child care.

mapping—technique used for communicating information about the physical environment. Maps may represent physical features such as land and climate conditions or abstract concepts such as *view corridors* and pedestrian *nodes*.

mass—combines all three dimensions (length, height, and depth). A building is often composed of many masses, hence the term *massing,* which is often used to describe the form or shape of structures like cathedrals.

masterplan—an overall plan for a specific area such as a downtown district, neighborhood, or waterfront that reflects community vision. A masterplan is more specific and detailed than a comprehensive plan.

mixed-use—a project or limited area of development which combines different land uses, such as housing, retail, and office uses.

National Historic Landmark (NHL)—buildings, historic districts, structures, sites, and objects that possess exceptional values or quality in illustrating or interpreting the heritage of the United States. The NHL program is run by the National Park Service, U.S. Department of the Interior.

National Register of Historic Places—the nation's official list of historic, architectural, archeological, and cultural resources. It is maintained by the National Park Service, U.S. Department of the Interior.

node—a hub of activity.

pedestrian flow—the direction and rate and frequency of pedestrian movement in an area.

pediment—the triangular face of a gable.

perspective—see *architectural drawings*

plan—see *architectural drawings*

planned unit development (PUD)—a form of development usually characterized by a unified site design for a number of housing units, clustering buildings and providing common open space; density increase; and a mix of building types and land uses. It permits the planning of a project and the calculation of densities over the entire development, rather than on an individual, lot-by-lot basis. It is usually administered through a special permit or zoning process.

pocket park—small, usually lot size, park in an urban area.

preservation—providing for the continued use of deteriorated old and historic buildings, sites, structures, and objects. The means for preservation include restoration, rehabilitation, and adaptive use. According to the Secretary of the Interior, it is "the act or process of applying measures to sustain the existing form, integrity, and material of a building or structure, and the existing form and vegetative cover of the site. It may include stabilization work, where necessary, as well as ongoing maintenance of the historic building materials."

preserve—a vulnerable area protected from development, such as a natural area or an agricultural area.

proportion—the ratio or relative size of two or more dimensions. The term can be used to refer to the ratio of the width to the height of a door or window opening, or to the ratio of the width of a building to its height.

public art—expenditure of public funds for artwork that is used to create a space or viewed as an object, temporary or permanent, participatory or not. Such art can broaden perceptions about the physical environment.

ratio of solid to void—the solid-to-void relationship refers to the proportions between the total area of wall surface area and the area of "holes" (i.e., windows, doors, arches, etc.) of a building. This relationship determines the appearance of a building in a very basic way, with the range of possibilities extending from a stone fortress to a glass house.

reconstruction—the act or process of reproducing by new construction the exact form and detail of a vanished building, structure, or object, or a part thereof, as it appeared at a specific period of time.

rehabilitation—the act or process of returning a property to a state of utility through repair or alteration which makes possible an efficient contemporary use while preserving those portions or features of the property which are significant to its historical, architectural, and cultural values.

renovation—modernization of an old or historic structure. Unlike restoration, renovation may not be consistent with the original design.

restoration—the act or process of accurately recovering the form and details of a property and its setting as it appeared at a particular period of time by means of the removal of later work or by the replacement of missing earlier work.

RFP (Request for proposal)—a written set of guidelines used in soliciting proposals from consultants, architects, developers, artists, and other contractors.

RFQ (Request for qualifications)—a call for qualifications such as a résumé, portfolio, and project list.

rhythm and pattern—relate to materials, styles, shapes, and spacing of building elements and the buildings themselves. The predominance of one material or shape, and its patterns of recurrence, are characteristics of an area that need to be maintained.

scale—the apparent size of a building, window, or other element as perceived in relation to the size of a human being. Scale refers to the apparent size, not actual size, since it is always viewed in relationship to another building or element. For instance, the scale of one element may be altered simply by changing the size of an element nearby, such as windows, doors, or other architectural details. These relationships contribute to the experience of a place as intimate, vast, "larger than life," and daunting, etc.

scenic corridor—a strip of land on each side of a stream or roadway that is generally visible to the public traveling on such route, or a roadway that has a view of unusual natural significance in a community.

scenic easement—a public agency obtains use of private land for scenic enhancement, such as roadside landscaping and vista point preservation.

section—see *architectural drawings*

Section 106—provision of the National Historic Preservation Act of 1966 which requires the head of a federal agency financing or licensing a project to determine the effect of the project on property in or eligible for the *National Register of Historic Places.*

sense of place—the feeling associated with a location, based on a unique identity and other memorable qualities.

setback—zoning code standard for locating a building or structure at a minimum distance (set back) from a street or lot line.

sign ordinance—a legal mechanism for controlling the design, size, height, etc. of signs.

site plan—a plan prepared to scale, showing accurately and with complete dimensioning the boundaries of a site and the location of all buildings, structures, uses, and principal site design features proposed for a specific parcel of land.

sprawl—dispersed development over large areas of landscape.

stabilization—the act or process of applying measures designed to re-establish a weather resistant enclosure and the structural stability of unsafe or deteriorated property while maintaining the essential form as it exists at present.

street furniture—municipal equipment placed along streets, including light fixtures, fire hydrants, police and fire call boxes, trash receptacles, signs, benches, newspaper boxes, and kiosks.

streetscape—the distinguishing character of a particular street as created by its width, degree of curvature, paving materials, design of the street furniture, and forms of surrounding buildings.

subdivision—the process of laying out a parcel of raw land into lots, blocks, streets, and public areas. Its purpose is the transformation of raw land into building sites. in most states, a subdivision is defined as the division of a tract of land into five or more lots.

survey of cultural resources—see *inventory*

townscape—the relationship of buildings, shapes, spaces, and textures that gives a town or area its distinctive visual character or image.

transfer of development rights (TDR)—a system of land development control wherein rights, or development units, are assigned to each parcel of land based upon planning studies and density control factors. These rights are separable and may be transferred to other parcels; thus they are marketable. Once the development right is transferred, a restriction on development will run with the land. TDRs have frequently been used to protect agricultural land and permit increased density in targeted areas.

transition space—see *edge*

transparency—refers to the interaction between an observer and an activity in an environment. It allows the observer to "read" what is happening inside a structure or in another area. For example, a commercial building is considered transparent if the pedestrian can view the merchandise or interior activity from the street.

universal design—design which is accessible to "all" people, regardless of age, disability, etc.

urban limit line—development boundary used to protect rural or agricultural lands from encroaching urban development.

vernacular—landscape or architectural style common to, or representative of, an area.

view corridor—refers to the line of vision from an observation point to a viewpoint, often used in determining scenic easements.

wetland—a freshwater or saltwater marsh. In technical terms, the U.S. government definition is based on soil type and vegetative species.

zoning—dividing an area into sections determined by specific restrictions on land use or types of construction. *Downzoning* and *upzoning* are changes in the zoning code which allow more (upzoning) or less (downzoning) intensive uses or densities than previously prescribed. *Euclidean* is the traditional zoning practice which hierarchically ranks uses, with housing as the highest use and manufacturing as the lowest. As seen in suburban development, Euclidean zoning tends to separate uses. *Incentive* zoning uses bonus credits which allow more intensive use of land in exchange for providing one or more amenities, such as density bonus in exchange for open space. An *overlay* is a special purpose zone which is overlaid on the city's general zoning map. The overlay zone designates applicable areas for special condition or use, including historic districts. *Performance* zoning uses flexible regulations based upon performance standards. In order to mitigate street noise in a house, restrictive zoning might stipulate minimum setback requirements. Performance zoning would state a minimum acceptable noise level in the front room of a house and permit creative solutions to solve the problem.

Sources

American Planning Association. *A Survey of Zoning Definitions.* Planning Advisory Service, Report Number 421.

Hedman, Richard. *Fundamentals of Urban Design.* Chicago: American Planning Association, 1984.

Lynch, Kevin. *The Image of the City.* Boston: MIT Press, 1977.

Lyndon, Donlyn. *The City Observed: Boston.* New York: Vintage Books, 1982.

Mackin, Anne, and Alex Krieger. *A Design Primer for Cities and Towns.* Massachusetts Council on the Arts and Humanities, 1989.

National Trust for Historic Preservation. *The Yellow Pages.*

Portland, Oregon. *Central City Plan.* Portland: Bureau of Planning, 1988.

Smith, Herbert. *The Citizens Guide to Planning.* Chicago: American Planning Association, 1979.

Smith, Herbert. *The Citizens Guide to Zoning.* Chicago: American Planning Association, 1983.

Solnit, Albert. *The Job of the Planning Commissioner.* Chicago: American Planning Association, 1987.

Vineyard Open Land Foundation. *Looking at the Vineyard,* 1973.

NOTES

1. Malvina Reynolds, "Little Boxes," Copyright © 1962 by Schroder Music Company (ASCAP), Berkeley, California, renewed 1990. Copyright approval for reproduction of Reynolds' quote in this book by Schroder Music Company gratefully acknowledged by the author.

2. The four points of the Main Street Program include design, organization, economic development, and promotion.

3. *ReVision 2000—Take Charge Again,* Chattanooga, Tennessee: Chattanooga Venture, 1993.

4. Key participants in this project who contributed to this list of factors include Ann Hershfang, Ken Kruckemeyer, and Tony Pangaro.

5. Source: Kenneth Kruckemeyer, Massachusetts Department of Public Works. Calculations based on 4,000 square feet of bridge surface at $200 per square foot construction costs, plus related expenses.

6. My partner for all of the bridge design work was Ken Kruckemeyer, then the Associate Commissioner of the Massachusetts Department of Public Works. His experience as an architect, public official, and community activist was important to the success of the program.

7. Adele Fleet Bacow and Kenneth Kruckemeyer, editors, *Bridge Design: Aesthetics and Developing Technologies,* Massachusetts Department of Public Works and the Massachusetts Council on the Arts and Humanities, 1986, p. 67.

8. Ann Myers Hershfang, "The Beautification of the Massachusetts Turnpike," *Radcliffe Quarterly* (March 1993): 17–18.

9. *Places as Art* provides a creative approach to viewing the city environment. Produced by Maguire/Reeder, Ltd., it is available through the National Endowment for the Arts' Design Arts Program.

10. Rebecca A. Lee and Associates, *Spurring the Creation of Artists' Live/Work Space in Massachusetts*, A Report to the Massachusetts Council on the Arts and Humanities, 1987, p. 6.

11. ArtsMarket Consulting, Inc. "Cultural Facilities Needs Study Conducted for the Massachusetts Industrial Finance Agency," August 21, 1989, pp. 1–2.

12. "Cultural Facilities Fund," a project of the Nonprofit Cultural Facilities Fund, New York, 1993.

13. Parts of this chapter were drawn from the article written by Adele Fleet Bacow and Mary Jane Daly, "The People Choose: Governor's

Design Awards Program of Massachusetts," published in *Place*, Vol. 8, No. 2, March–April 1988.

14. Examples drawn from Mayors Institute on City Design newsletter, *City Design,* and staff summaries.

15. Denise A. Bell and Elijuh Mirochnik, *A Guidebook to Selected Projects in Design Education*, Boston: Massachusetts Council on the Arts and Humanities, 1989, p. 1.

16. Anne Taylor, George Vlastos, and Alison Marshall, *Architecture and Children—Core Curriculum, Posters, and Teachers Guide,* Albuquerque, New Mexico: School Zone Institute, 1991.

17. American Institute of Architects, *The Search for Excellence in Architecture-in-Schools,* Washington, D.C.: The Environmental Education Program of the American Institute of Architects, 1988.

18. The information contained in this summary was obtained by surveying the Design Arts Program of each state arts council in the country and from the Design Access data base of the National Endowment for the Arts. The programs cited are funded by appropriations from the individual state legislatures and by grants from the National Endowment for the Arts.

SELECTED BIBLIOGRAPHY

Literature

Abhau, Marcy, editor, with Rolaine Copeland and Greta Greenberger. *Architecture In Education: A Resource of Imaginative Ideas and Tested Activities.* Philadelphia, Pennsylvania: Foundation for Architecture, 1986.

American Institute of Architects. *The Search for Excellence in Architecture-in-Schools.* Washington, D.C.: The Environmental Education Program of the American Institute of Architects, 1988.

Arendt, Randall, with E. Brabec, H. Dodson, C. Reid, and R. Yaro. *Rural by Design: Maintaining Small Town Character.* Chicago, Illinois: American Planning Association, 1994.

Arts Market Consulting, Inc. "Cultural Facilities Needs Study Conducted for the Massachusetts Industrial Finance Agency." Boston, Massachusetts: Massachusetts Industrial Finance Agency, August 21, 1989.

Babize, Mollie, and Walter Cudnohufsky. *Designing Your Corner of Vermont.* Montpelier, Vermont: Vermont Council on the Arts, 1991.

Bacow, Adele Fleet. *Broadening Our Vision: Connecting the Arts and Community Development.* Cambridge, Massachusetts: New England Foundation for the Arts, 1993.

Bacow, Adele Fleet, and Mary Jane Daly. "The People Choose: Governor's Design Awards Program of Massachusetts," *Place,* Vol. 8, No. 2, March–April 1988.

Bacow, Adele Fleet, and Kenneth Kruckemeyer, editors. *Bridge Design: Aesthetics and Developing Technology.* Boston, Massachusetts: Massachusetts Department of Public Works and Massachusetts Council on the Arts and Humanities, 1986.

Barnett, Jonathan. *An Introduction to Urban Design.* New York: Harper and Row, 1982.

Beatty, Paula, editor-in-chief. *Community Design Book.* Oklahoma City, Oklahoma: State Arts Council of Oklahoma, 1993.

Beaumont, Constance E. *How Superstore Sprawl Can Harm Communities—And What Citizens Can Do About It.* Washington, D.C.: National Trusts for Historic Preservation, 1994.

Bell, Denise, and Elijuh Mirochnik. *A Guidebook to Selected Projects in Design Education.* Boston, Massachusetts: Massachusetts Council on the Arts and Humanities, 1989.

Brown, Catherine R., William Fleissig, and William Morrish. *Building for the Arts.* Santa Fe, New Mexico: Western States Arts Federation, 1989.

Centerbrook Architects and Planners. *Downtown Design Guidebook for Renovation and New Construction in Holyoke, Massachusetts.* Holyoke, Massachusetts: City of Holyoke, June 1988.

Craig, Lois, et al. *The Federal Presence: Architecture, Politics and National Design.* Cambridge, Massachusetts: MIT Press, 1978.

Cruikshank, Jeffrey L., and Pam Korza. *Going Public: A Field Guide to Developments in Art in Public Places.* Amherst, Massachusetts: Arts Extension Service of the University of Massachusetts, 1987.

Frieden, Bernard, and Lynne Sagalyn. *Downtown, Inc.: How America Rebuilds Its Cities.* Cambridge, Massachusetts: MIT Press, 1990.

Gratz, Roberta. *The Living City—How America's Cities Are Being Revitalized by Thinking Small in a Big Way,* 2nd edition. Washington, D.C.: The Preservation Press, 1994.

Graves, Ginny, editor. *ArchiNEWS.* Newsletter on Built Environment Education. Prairie Village, Kansas: Center for Understanding the Built Environment, 1993.

Graves, Ginny, project coordinator. *Walk Around the Block.* Self-discovery workbook program for students and teachers to learn about their neighborhood. Prairie Village, Kansas: Center for Understanding the Built Environment, 1992.

Greene, Kevin W., editor. *The City as a Stage: Strategies for the Arts in Urban Economics.* Washington, D.C.: Partners for Livable Places, 1983.

Heder, Lajos, and Ellen Shoshkes. *Aesthetics in Transportation: Guidelines for Incorporating Design, Art and Architecture Into Transportation Facilities.* Washington, D.C.: U.S. Department of Transportation, 1980.

Hershfang, Ann Myers. "The Beautification of the Massachusetts Turnpike." *Radcliffe Quarterly* (March 1993): 17–18.

Isaacson, Philip M. *Round Buildings, Square Buildings, and Buildings that Wiggle Like a Fish.* New York: Alfred A. Knopf, Inc., 1988.

Jones, Bernie. *Neighborhood Planning: A Guide for Citizens and Planners.* Chicago, Illinois: American Planning Association, 1990.

Jones, Warren. *What Do I Do Next? A Manual for People Just Entering Government Service.* Washington, D.C.: Planners Press, 1980.

King, Stanley. *Co-Design: A Process of Design Participation.* New York: Van Nostrand Reinhold, 1989.

Klein, Richard D. *Everyone Wins! A Citizen's Guide to Development.* Washington, D.C.: American Planning Association, 1990.

Rebecca A. Lee and Associates. *Spurring the Creation of Artists' Live/Work Space in Massachusetts.* Boston, Massachusetts: Massachusetts Council on the Arts and Humanities, 1987.

Lynch, Kevin, and Gary Hack. *Site Planning.* Cambridge, Massachusetts: MIT Press, 1984.

Mackin, Anne. *Community Design—Six Case Studies of Cultural Revitalization.* Raleigh, North Carolina: North Carolina Arts Council, 1991.

Mackin, Anne. *Designing Your Town.* Washington, D.C.: American Institute of Architects, 1992.

Mackin, Anne, and Alex Krieger. *A Design Primer for Cities and Towns.* Boston, Massachusetts: Massachusetts Council on the Arts and Humanities, 1989.

Maine Arts Commission and University of Southern Maine. *The Hidden Design in Land Use Ordinances.* Portland, Maine: University of Southern Maine New England Studies, 1981.

Mantell, Michael A., Stephen F. Harper, and Luther Propst. *Creating Successful Communities: A Guidebook to Growth Management Strategies.* Washington, D.C.: The Conservation Foundation, Island Press, 1990.

Marcus, Clare Cooper, and Carolyn Francis, editors. *People Places: Design Guidelines for Urban Open Space.* New York: Van Nostrand Reinhold, 1990.

McNulty, Robert, et al. *The Economics of Amenity: Community Futures and Quality of Life.* Washington, D.C.: Partners for Livable Places, 1985.

Moudon, Anne Vernez. *Public Streets for Public Use.* New York: Van Nostrand Reinhold, 1987.

Nelson, Doreen. *Transformations—Process and Theory: A Curriculum Guide to Creative Development.* Santa Monica, California: Center for City Building Educational Programs, 1984.

New England Foundation for the Arts. *The Arts and the New England Economy.* Cambridge, Massachusetts: New England Foundation for the Arts, 1980.

Page, Clint, and Penelope Cuff. *The Public Sector Designs.* Washington, D.C.: Partners for Livable Places, 1984.

Partners for Livable Places. *The Better Community Catalogue: A Sourcebook of Ideas, People and Strategies for Improving the Place Where You Live.* Washington, D.C.: Acropolis Books, Ltd., 1989.

Porter, Robert, editor. *Arts Advocacy: A Citizen Action Manual.* Washington, D.C.: American Council for the Arts, 1980.

Porter, Robert, editor. *The Arts and City Planning.* New York: American Council for the Arts, 1980.

Radich, Anthony J. *Design Decisionmaking in the States.* Denver, Colorado: National Conference of State Legislatures, 1984.

Ramati, Raquel. *How to Save Your Own Streets.* Garden City, New York: Dolphin Books, 1981.

ReVision 2000—Take Charge Again. Chattanooga, Tennessee: Chattanooga Venture, 1993.

Rypkema, Donovan D. *The Economics of Historic Preservation—A Community Leader's Guide.* Washington, D.C.: National Trust for Historic Preservation, 1994.

Schuster, Mark Davidson, editor. *The Arts and Urban Development: Four Case Studies.* Cambridge, Massachusetts: MIT Center for Real Estate Development, 1988.

Scrimger, Kay Randle. *How Mayors and City Governments Support the Arts: Innovative Financing Techniques and Strategies.* Washington, D.C.: The United States Conference of Mayors, 1988.

Shirvani, Hamid. *The Urban Design Process.* New York: Van Nostrand Reinhold, 1985.

Shoshkes, Ellen. *The Design Process.* New York: Whitney Library of Design, 1989.

Snedcof, Howard R. *Cultural Facilities in Mixed-Use Development.* Washington, D.C.: The Urban Land Institute, 1985.

Stokes, Samuel N., and Elizabeth Watson. *Saving America's Countryside: A Guide to Rural Conservation.* Baltimore: The John Hopkins University Press, 1989.

Taylor, Anne, George Vlastos, and Alison Marshall. *Architecture and Children—Core Curriculum, Posters, and Teacher's Guide.* Albuquerque, New Mexico: School Zone Institute, 1991.

U.S. Department of Housing and Urban Development. *Lessons from Local Experience.* Washington, D.C.: U.S. Government Printing Office, 1983.

Ward, Janet, editor. "Public Works Become Public Art." *American City and County,* September 1993.

Whyte, William H. *City: Rediscovering the Center.* New York: Doubleday, 1989.

Whyte, William H. *The Social Life of Small Urban Spaces.* Washington, D.C.: The Conservation Foundation, 1980.

Yaro, Robert D., et al., and Center for Rural Massachusetts. *Dealing with Change in the Connecticut River Valley: A Design Manual for Conserva-*

tion and Development. Cambridge, Massachusetts: Lincoln Institute for Land Policy, 1988.

Videotapes

Cambridge Studios. *Creating Artists' Space.* Boston, Massachusetts: Massachusetts Council on the Arts and Humanities.

Cambridge Studios. *Gateway of Color* (video on the MassPike Bridge Design Project). Boston, Massachusetts: Massachusetts Turnpike Authority.

Maguire/Reeder, Ltd. *Design Competitions.* Washington, D.C.: National Endowment for the Arts, Design Arts Program.

Maguire/Reeder, Ltd. *Looking at Change Before It Occurs.* Washington, D.C.: National Endowment for the Arts, Design Arts Program (videotape on computer visual simulation and community design).

Maguire/Reeder, Ltd. *Places As Art.* Washington, D.C.: National Endowment for the Arts.

Monadnock Media, Inc. *Growing Smart—A Practical Alternative to Haphazard Growth in Massachusetts.* Amherst, Massachusetts: Center for Rural Massachusetts.

National Trust for Historic Preservation, Washington, D.C., *Main Street at Work:* Separate videotapes entitled *Bringing in Business; Getting Organized; Investing in Your Image; Keeping Up Appearances; The Main Street Approach;* and *Main Street at Work.*

INDEX

About the Author

Adele Fleet Bacow is a distinguished urban planner specializing in community economic development, design, and the arts. She holds a bachelor of arts degree in urban design from Wellesley College and a master's degree in city planning from the Massachusetts Institute of Technology.

Over the past twenty years Ms. Bacow has brought together the public and private sectors in unlikely collaborations to revitalize communities. Formerly director of design and development at the Massachusetts Council on the Arts and Humanities, she won a Presidential Design Achievement Award for her work described in this book. Ms. Bacow also served as deputy director of the Massachusetts Government Land Bank and coordinator of the Mayors Institute on City Design. She consults nationally on projects relating to community development, urban design, and the arts. Currently senior vice president of the consulting firm Policy and Management Associates, Inc., in Boston, she lives in Newton, Massachusetts, with her husband and two sons.